*Routledge Revivals*

# English Usage

First published in 1986, this book examines the changing patterns in English usage and style. It encourages a constructive attitude to language, demonstrating the creative resources of grammar, discussing in detail the options of written style, and challenging the authoritarian spirit that inhibits usage. The central chapters are concerned with written usage, and pay close attention to questions of syntax and punctuation. The sense of writing, however, is always related to speech, and the value of usage as a social act is emphasised in the exploration of style as an individual function. Technical terms are explained and the text is illustrated with examples from literature and journalism.

# English Usage
## A Guide to First Principles

### Walter Nash

Routledge
Taylor & Francis Group

First published in 1986
by Routledge & Kegan Paul

This edition first published in 2017 by Routledge
2 Park Square, Milton Park, Abingdon, Oxon, OX14 4RN
and by Routledge
711 Third Avenue, New York, NY 10017

*Routledge is an imprint of the Taylor & Francis Group, an informa business*

© 1986 Walter Nash

All rights reserved. No part of this book may be reprinted or reproduced or utilised in any form or by any electronic, mechanical, or other means, now known or hereafter invented, including photocopying and recording, or in any information storage or retrieval system, without permission in writing from the publishers.

**Publisher's Note**
The publisher has gone to great lengths to ensure the quality of this reprint but points out that some imperfections in the original copies may be apparent.

**Disclaimer**
The publisher has made every effort to trace copyright holders and welcomes correspondence from those they have been unable to contact.

A Library of Congress record exists under LC control number: 8514506

ISBN 13: 978-1-138-24236-4 (hbk)
ISBN 13: 978-1-315-27833-9 (ebk)
ISBN 13: 978-1-138-24243-2 (pbk)

# English Usage
## A guide to first principles

*Walter Nash*
*Department of English Studies*
*University of Nottingham*

Routledge & Kegan Paul
London, Boston and Henley

*First published in 1986
by Routledge & Kegan Paul plc*

*14 Leicester Square, London WC2H 7PH, England*

*9 Park Street, Boston, Mass. 02108, USA and*

*Broadway House, Newtown Road,
Henley on Thames, Oxon RG9 1EN, England*

*Set in 11 on 12 pt Times
by Inforum Ltd, Portsmouth
and printed in Great Britain
by T J Press (Padstow) Ltd
Padstow, Cornwall*

© *Walter Nash 1986*

*No part of this book may be reproduced in
any form without permission from the publisher,
except for the quotation of brief passages
in criticism*

*Library of Congress Cataloging-in-Publication Data*

*Nash, Walter.
English usage.
(Language, education, and society)
Bibliography: p.
Includes index
1. English language—Rhetoric. 2. English language—
Usage. 3. English language—Style. I. Title.
II. Series.
PE1408.N24    1986    808'.042    85-14506
British Library CIP data also available*

*ISBN 0-7102-0024-2*

# Contents

| | | |
|---|---|---|
| | General editor's preface | vii |
| | Preface | xi |
| 1 | The usage trap | 1 |
| 2 | A little grammar: Styles of sentences | 15 |
| 3 | Prescriptions | 45 |
| 4 | Options | 73 |
| 5 | Punctuations | 100 |
| 6 | Authorities: Under which king? | 129 |
| | Bibliography | 158 |
| | Index | 162 |

> It is not the acquisition of any one thing
> that is able to adorn,
> or the incidental quality that occurs
> as a concomitant of something well said,
> that we value in style,
> but the principle that is hid . . .
>
> – Marianne Moore, 'To a Snail'

It were good therefore that men in their innovations would follow the example of time itself, which indeed innovateth greatly, but quietly and by degrees scarce to be perceived . . .

– Francis Bacon, 'Of Innovations'

# General editor's preface

Simply a list of some of the questions implied by the phrase *Language, Education and Society* gives an immediate idea of the complexity, and also the fascination, of the area.

How is language related to learning? Or to intelligence? How should a teacher react to non-standard dialect in the classroom? Do regional and social accents and dialects matter? What is meant by standard English? Does it make sense to talk of 'declining standards' in language or in education? Or to talk of some children's language as 'restricted'? Do immigrant children require special language provision? How can their native languages be used as a valuable resource in schools? Can 'literacy' be equated with 'education'? Why are there so many adult illiterates in Britain and the USA? What effect has growing up with no easy access to language: for example, because a child is profoundly deaf? Why is there so much prejudice against people whose language background is odd in some way: because they are handicapped, or speak a non-standard dialect or foreign language? Why do linguistic differences lead to political violence, in Belgium, India, Wales and other parts of the world?

These are all real questions, of the kind which worry parents, teachers and policy-makers, and the answer to them is complex and not at all obvious. It is such questions that authors in this series will discuss.

Language plays a central part in education. This is probably generally agreed, but there is considerable debate and confusion about the exact relationship between language and learning. Even though the importance of language is generally recognized, we still have a lot to learn about how language is related either to educational success or to intelligence and thinking. Language is also a central fact in everyone's social life. People's attitudes and most deeply held beliefs are at stake, for it is through language that personal and social identities are maintained and recognized. People are judged, whether justly or not, by the language they speak.

*Language, education and society* is therefore an area where scholars have a responsibility to write clearly and persuasively, in order to communicate the best in recent research to as wide an audience as possible. This means not only other researchers, but also all those who are involved in educational, social and political policy-making, from individual teachers to government. It is an area where value judgments cannot be avoided. Any action that we take – or, of course, avoidance of action – has moral, social and political consequences. It is vital, therefore, that practice is informed by the best knowledge available, and that decisions affecting the futures of individual children or whole social groups are not taken merely on the basis of the all too widespread folk myths about language in society.

Linguistics, psychology and sociology are often rejected by non-specialists as jargon-ridden; or regarded as fascinating, but of no relevance to educational or social practice. But this is superficial and short-sighted: we are dealing with complex issues, which require an understanding of the general principles involved. It is bad theory to make statements about language in use which cannot be related to educational and social reality. But it is equally unsound to base beliefs and action on anecdote, received myths and unsystematic or idiosyncratic observations.

All knowledge is value-laden: it suggests action and changes our beliefs. Change is difficult and slow, but possible nevertheless. When language in education and society is seriously and systematically studied, it becomes clear how awesomely complex is the linguistic and social knowledge of all children and adults. And with such an understanding, it becomes impossible to maintain a position of linguistic prejudice and intolerance. This may be the most important implication of a serious study of language, in our linguistically diverse modern world.

Walter Nash's book tackles an important topic for this series:

a test case in some ways. Most people have their views on 'good English': but such views are often based on personal prejudice or received wisdom (or ignorance). Witness the demonstrable irrationality of complaining letters about pronunciation, style and usage which are sent to the BBC in their hundreds. They may be irrational in their arguments and ignorant of linguistic facts. It is not, however, irrational to worry about the issue itself: clear English is a valuable goal. And if people define a situation as important, it is important in its consequences.

It is a misunderstanding of a linguistic approach to think that it necessarily rejects prescriptivism. The real objection is to thoughtless prescriptivism. Walter Nash described his book to me on one occasion as a 'thinking person's Strunk and White', referring to the enormously influential, and highly prescriptive, American manual of style. The merit of Nash's book is that it does not just make statements about questions of style, without argument. It contains a lot of good advice, but this is based both on interesting description of usage and also on contemporary sociolinguistic thinking about linguistic variation.

Many British linguists and other academics have derided the freshman creative writing courses found in American universities for their vague and muddled aims: 'courses in existential awareness and the accurate use of the comma', as Malcolm Bradbury calls them in one of his novels. In this book, Nash shows that it is possible to give advice which is both detailed and principled. The advice is also that of a practitioner. Nash is himself a gifted author and, as well as other books on language, he has published short stories and an extremely funny novel (*Kettle of Roses*, 1982).

Michael Stubbs
Nottingham

# Preface

I once had the notion of calling this book a guide *for the time being*; the phrase actually remains in its final sentence, the fossil of a discarded intention. 'For the time being' was to be read in a double sense. I supposed, in the first place, that serious students of usage and style might find the book helpful as a first step towards more advanced studies; and in the second place I wished to acknowledge my own limitations – as indeed I still do. For the time being, these chapters represent all that I can usefully say on a very complex topic.

During the course of composition, I became aware of a third sense lurking in this key phrase. As I consulted various Usages published during the last eighty years, it struck me that books of this kind may be called political acts, to the extent that they appeal to a favoured, socially stable class of right-thinking people, whose assumptions they both inform and confirm. Because their authors have seldom if ever recognized openly the social implications of their work, Usages have become almost an artificial genre, handing down their encapsulated dogmas, losing touch with usage and users, losing touch with time, stiffly ignoring the need for the social philosophy of language which should irradiate such books. I say *should*; alas, I cannot claim to have supplied the defect on my own behalf, or to have done more than indicate (notably in my final chapter) an awareness of what is generally wrong with this species of text. I should like to attempt a new kind of Usage; but for the time being, I have composed one along more or less traditional lines.

At the outset, I proposed to write a very short text comprising a few basic prescriptions for written usage. The model proposed to me (but not by my present editor and publisher) was W. Strunk and E.B. White's *The Elements of Style*. This undertaking, the remains of which can be traced in my Chapter 3, confirmed for me what I already knew about the limitations of the *prescriptive*. I began to expand the scope of the book by essaying a broadly *descriptive* text, which could easily have run into several exhaustive (or exhausting) volumes. Signs of this effort are apparent in Chapter 2, an attempt to review the principal resources of English grammar in relationship to questions of style. At length it became clear to me that the aim of a work of this kind should be neither prescriptive nor ambitiously descriptive, but *constructive*; that is, that I should try to demonstrate and discuss helpfully the stylistic choices available to the user of English. This discussion, contained for the most part in Chapters 4 and 5, relates mainly to problems of written Engish. A final stage in composition I have already mentioned; in my Chapters 1 and 6 – the framing chapters of the work – I raise questions of usage in the general context of language and society. Chapter 6 in particular may appear to be severely critical of some venerated authorities. I must therefore insist that it is by no means my intention to be destructive (whoever writes about language lives in a glass house), but only to suggest that we should question conventional wisdoms, even to the extent of thoroughly revising our ideas of how problems of usage should be propounded and solved.

This description of the book's progress through stages of composition may suggest a haphazard and planless growth. I naturally hope that reading will dispel any such impression. An argument is developed from chapter to chapter, and is supported as fully as possible by illustrations. Some of these are of my own invention; some are taken from newspapers and journals (the source is in all cases acknowledged); and in one or two instances, wishing to indicate how 'usage' touches the extremes of casual colloquy and literary art, I have used passages of fiction or expository prose. I am sure that in developing my theme I have overlooked matters which many readers will think I should have treated; and I am equally sure that in many places I have sinned against principles of sound usage, even against principles I have myself endorsed. This is the destiny of all who dare to tell language what to do. We are apprenticed to fallibility.

## Preface

In Chapters 1–5, quotations from literary and other works are furnished with details in full of title and author. In Chapter 6, where continual reference is made to a number of books on usage, I have adopted a system of abbreviated reference, by letter and number, which is clarified in the prefatory note to the Bibliography. The latter is a brief list of books on usage, style, rhetoric, and related matters. Some of these works are discussed in my text; others are listed, with brief annotations, for their potential value to students of this subject.

It only remains to thank those who have helped me to bring this book into being. My greatest debt is certainly Michael Stubbs, a shrewdly perceptive and mercifully patient editor. I owe Ronald Carter my thanks for his tactful encouragement, particularly at a time when I was inclined to put the work aside as an irredeemable miscalculation; and for their kindness in reading and commenting invaluably on an early draft of the manuscript, I must express my appreciation to Geoffrey Leech and Mick Short. These were the sponsors of my work; and theirs will be a great measure of the credit if, on going out into the world, it makes friends.

University of Nottingham      WN

# 1
# The usage trap

'This boy calls the knaves jacks.'

– Estella, in Charles Dickens, *Great Expectations*

Reactions still triggered off by the sound of a vowel, the cut of a coat, the turn of a phrase. . . Once imbued with such reactions it is impossible to escape them; I know that until the day I die I shall be unable to escape noticing 'raound' for 'round', 'invoalve' for 'involve' (on that one an Army officer of my acquaintance used to turn down candidates for a commission).

– Diana Athill, *Instead of a Letter*

CONDITIONAL CLAUSES have always caused trouble to the semi-educated and the demi-reflective; to the illiterate they give no trouble at all. Most well-educated and well-speaking persons have little difficulty.

– Eric Partridge, *Usage and Abusage*

And so the upstart is put in his place, ambition is repressed, the meritorious sheep are distinguished from the barely deserving goats. How disagreeable these pronouncements are, and how embarrassing! – for few will read without a pang of misgiving the quotations that head this chapter. We are all inclined to judge others by their language, but we like to suppose that our comments are strictly fair and reasonable; the suspicion that in some matters we might be every bit as snobbish, reactionary, or pedantic as the worst of our authoritarian neighbours is disconcerting. But are these crude acts of discrimination inevitable? Or can we, recognizing in ourselves the only-human habit of being right, learn to temper our dislikes, to make honestly reasoned observations, to counter prejudice with constructive argument? That question represents the theme of this book. We are to consider problems of usage and principles of style, but above all else we must try to understand how language is at our creative disposal; and how only by exploring its resources do we begin to free ourselves from the *usage trap*, that prescriptive snare that disables and confines the rule-giver as effectively as it intimidates the ruled.

## 1 Speaking and writing

Let us first look at a commonly received idea: that speaking is a debased activity, necessarily inferior to writing. This belief was firmly held in the eighteenth century, a time when men of letters were anxious to see the language 'fixed' in secure, correct, and durable forms. Here, for instance, is Dr Johnson on the theme of conversation versus composition:

> A transition from an author's books to his conversation is too often like an entrance into a large city, after a distant prospect. Remotely, we see nothing but spires of temples, and turrets of palaces, and imagine it to be the residence of splendour, grandeur, and magnificence; but, when we have passed the gates, we find it perplexed with narrow passages, disgraced with despicable cottages, embarrassed with obstructions and clouded with smoke.
> (*The Rambler*, no 14, 5 May 1750)

The imagery of architecture (making language the 'edifice' of thought) typifies the classical view of composition. Nouns of large compass (*splendour grandeur, magnificence*) suggest the scope of creative design in writing; participles denoting merely human predicaments (*perplexed, disgraced, embarrassed*) criticize the muddle of speech. Order and permanence are the virtues Johnson has in prospect, and he sees them in well-tutored, well-housed Composition, not in semi-educated, alley-dwelling Conversation.

The gross unfairness of this is that the image is allowed to dictate the terms of the argument. All that Johnson is really saying is that an author has time to plan his writing, to consider its structure and refine its style; whereas when he enters into conversation he must do the best he can to meet the demands of the fleeting moment, and act his part in situations which he cannot wholly control. This does not mean that speech is a form of linguistic jerrybuilding. It implies that there are techniques of writing and somewhat different techniques of speaking – different, but nonetheless governed by ascertainable principles. The notion of principle and technique in spoken language, however, is alien to the authoritarian spirit. Does not the very etymology of the word *grammar* – *grammatikē tekhnē* – denote 'the art of *letters*'? There is a rooted belief that if speech has any design, any resemblance to a style, it is by derivation from writing. The progression suggested in the *Rambler* passage is significant. A move is made from books to conversation, measuring the inadequacies of speech by the fixed standard of writing; not from conversation to books, discovering the peculiar features in which writing must differ from speech.

Such attitudes, long ingrained, encourage the assumption that in speech and conversation a *style* is hardly possible, or is available only in the form of a deliberate bookishness. Whenever criteria of acceptability or 'correctness' are applied to speech, it is seldom with the primary aim of promoting communication and effective discourse; nearly always, the object is *social* acceptability, the correct behaviour of a class, a coterie, a generation. The effect of this is stultifying. If you dissociate the study of speech from its proper connection with the study of creativeness in language, you allow it to become a mere adjunct of genteel nurture, like etiquette or discreet tailoring. You make a word a blow to self-esteem; you let a man's vowels decide whether he is fit to hold a commission.

At the same time you complicate the difficulties of written language, because to affirm the status of writing as a higher thing than speech, an exacting craft, a linguistic attainment beyond the scope of the 'semi-educated' and the 'demi-reflective', you must burden it with delicate rules and quasi-regulations. You may decide, for instance, that sentences ought not to begin with *and* (this book begins and ends with such sentences); or that *tolerant to* is 'incorrect', an aberration from *tolerant of*; that *whilst* is obsolete; that *when . . . ever* (as in *When did Americans ever flinch from the truth?*) is a misuse of *whenever*; that *such a(n)*, as in *He was criticized for inventing such an unbelievable character*, is a dubious idiom, the preferred construction being *He was criticized for inventing so unbelievable a character*, or *for inventing a character so unbelievable*. These examples, all but one taken from a reputable manual, typify the prescriptive spirits that makes the usage trap. The rule-giver becomes inordinately sensitive to vagaries of expression; he seeks out deviations that allegedly impair communication or reflect imprecision of thought. But it is rare for such pronouncements to be truly relevant to an efficient use of language. They are often like superstitions, to be observed for fear of incurring the penalty of some nameless curse. They do little to support the would-be writer; on the contrary, they complicate the problems of putting pen to paper.

## 2 Usage and style

To contrast speaking with writing is to imply other oppositions: of the community, negotiating *usage* through collaborative exchanges, and the individual, self-communing, shaping a *style* in isolation. First thoughts on the subject suggest these correlations:

```
Speaking  ———————  Writing
   |                    |
Community ———————  Individual
   |                    |
'Usage'   ———————   'Style'
```

But this is faulty in at least one respect, its restriction of usage to *speaking*. Usage surely means the consensus of practice in using language, whether in conversation or composition; it is a notion that embraces both modes of verbal activity, implying complementation rather than contrast:

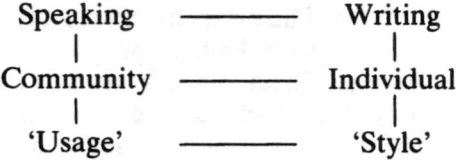

Spoken idiom is adopted into writing through the naturalizing agency of correspondence, of newspapers, of advertisements, of all kinds of public communication; while in its turn writing influences many varieties of speech. As users of the language we learn to assess current conditions. Our judgments tell us that a particular expression is appropriate to speech, but perhaps not to writing; or to informal communication but not to formal exchanges; or that it belongs to writing rather than to speech; or that it is acceptable in writing and speech alike.

These judgments are related to a view of the individual and the community. The personality is not, after all, so mechanically constructed that we can firmly distinguish the effects and products of 'individual' experience from those of 'communal' interactions. The roles of private being and social being overlap. Then from this commerce of individual with community, and from the complementation of written usage and spoken usage, *styles* emerge; styles of creative individuals, writing, in isolation from their fellows, yet always conscious of community, interaction, speech; style of socially effective speakers, in company, bound to the passing moment, improvising, yet aware of individuality, of design, of linguistic resources drawn from the practice of writing. Modes of writing and speaking are subject to change. Usage changes continually, and irresistibly, though we may think all change is for the worse; and with changes in usage come gradual modifications in style and in views of style. Samuel Johnson, a classical writer with a hankering of lapidary permanence in language, knew about linguistic change, recognized the futility of trying to prevent it, and expressed his insight in a much-quoted sentence: 'To enchain syllables, and to lash the wind, are alike the undertakings of pride, unwilling to measure its desire by its strength.' The warning stands, for all writers on usage to heed.

### 3 Language on the move

One very good reason for not huffing *pro*scriptions and puffing *pre*scriptions is that time and chance are liable to blow your house down. Swift angrily dismissed *nowadays* as a piece of modish cant; but nowadays everyone says *nowadays* (apart from wretches who prefer to say *at this moment in time*). Reading Eric Partridge's strictures on the expression *present-day* (which, in 1947, he condemned as an 'unnecessary synonym' for *present* or *contemporary*), I reflect a little sheepishly on my own tetchy resistance to our telecasters' *modern-day*, which seems to me abominable usurper of good old honest *present-day*. Time rings in the new words – rings in *nowadays*, rings in *modern-day*, rings in *telecaster*; and is not to be reasoned with. Dr Johnson was right; you cannot fetter a phrase, or manacle a manner of speaking.

There are changes in language which are readily understood, and which allow of scholarly explanations. With a little knowledge of phonetics and articulatory processes, we can interpret some changes in pronunciation. Acquaintance with the system of grammar, as a way of representing modes of perception and cognition, may help us to account for certain changes in syntax; we can see how similar constructions are confused, how one grammatical pattern develops analogously from another, how the struggle to express distinct perceptions leads to the creation or modification of syntactic resources. Our vocabulary, too, is demonstrably the product of cultural and psychological rulings. Scholars can show us how the meanings of words are changed or extended, how new words are brought into being, how one word usurps another, how there is such economy in language that no two words in living use can have exactly the same value.

All such changes – documented, classified, studied in the light of linguistic principle, psychological motive, historical fact – can be related to some sort of unifying hypothesis. They suggest a science, or at least a plausibly reflective account, of language on the move, in its slow budgings and re-alignings. But some usages are too close to us, too intimately bound up with personal experience, too fragmentary, too *complex* in being so close and so brokenly perceived, for us to be able to relate them to anything as cool and scientific as a hypothesis. They hardly enter into our experience as knowledge; they are more appropriately compared with gossip.

## 4 The gossip of change

Consider, for a digressive page or two, some personal examples of this 'gossip' of change. My father always called the knaves *jacks*; but my mother, who had been a domestic servant in a well-to-do household, never called them anything other than *knaves*. Moreover, she consistently referred to *court cards*, whereas my father said *face cards* (much to her amusement). They both pronounced the word *advertisement* with the accent on the third syllable, and stressed *controversy* on the second. My father pronounced *launch* and *staunch* to rhyme with southern British English *ranch*, having acquired the habit, I always supposed, from the naval personnel he met during the course of his work in a shipyard; if taxed or teased about it, he would reply that he was speaking the King's English – the king in question being George V.

Whenever my mother *laid*, or my father *set*, the table, they would put out *serviettes*. My mother, whose formal education ended at the age of eight, regularly mismanaged certain constructions, notably the relative clause: *I was going to pay the coalman last Saturday, which I might say he didn't come, so I couldn't*. My father, who left his grammar school at the age of twelve, could deftly negotiate all hazards of syntax, and had been instructed with such punitive rigour that he never, to the best of my remembrance, made a spelling error. My mother's use of language was vivid and original. She invented words to compensate for her occasional want of standard dictionary items (*teapotliddous* = 'vapid', 'inane'; *tittybottlous* = 'infantile', 'pusillanimous'); made frequent use of robust if somewhat opaque similes (*daft as a wagon horse; black as Dick's hatband*); and had a blunt way with bleak facts (*he's about ready for his box* and *another clean shirt'll do him both* = 'he will soon be dead'). My father liked 'fine' words (never a *beginning* if an *inception* could be arranged), and, when moved, dearly loved a literary turn of phrase (habitually referring to the graveyard, for example, as *our last resting place*).

On the rare occasions when I play cards, I refer to the *jack* either as a *court card* or as a *face card*. *Knave* is for me a 'literary' word, to be used humorously or parodically (playing-card knaves go with *looking glasses* and *drawing rooms*; knaves in general are *scurvy* and wear wrinkled hose and greasy doublets). At school I was taught to accent the second syllable of *advertisement* and the first and third syllables of *controversy*. There I was also encouraged to rhyme *garage* with *barrage* (in my parents' pronunciation it rhymed with *marriage*). I stress the first and third syllables of *kilometre*, the first syllable of *harass*, and the last syllable of *cigarette*. I *set* the table, but if a guest arrives, I *lay* an extra place. Until I went to Cambridge, I followed my parents' example of referring to the serviceable *serviette*; thereafter I was tutored or teased into saying *table napkin*, a practice I have followed ever since. Having been educated (or institutionalized) at great length, I have got into my head enough grammar to replace demi-reflective difficulties with donnish dogma. I fret over constructions like *An honest man, the company trusted him completely*, which I would re-cast in the form *An honest man, he was completely trusted by the company* – maintaining this to be 'correct', even though hosts of scribes and mediamen would find no fault with the other. I am jealous to preserve into age what I learned in my youth, becoming irritable when *refute* appears as a synonym of 'deny', when *cohort* is used as though it meant 'accomplice' or 'colleague' (*Mr X, one of President Reagan's cohorts*), when *momentarily* is made to bear the sense of 'soon', 'at any moment', 'in a few minutes' (*We are approaching London, and will be landing at Heathrow momentarily*).

My pupils nearly all call the knaves *jacks*, refer generally to *serviettes*, and are amused by the bourgeois pretensions of my *table napkin*. They rhyme *garage* with *marriage*, as my parents did ('garahges' are for Rolls-Royces, 'garridges' for demotic Fords and family runabouts), and are in two minds about the accentuation of *cigarette*, shrewdly noting the effect of phrase- or clause-rhythm (e.g. in *Cígarettes are déar* vs *I smóked a cigarétte*). They are sensitive to the use of gender-suffixes and gender pronouns: *chairpersons* rule, and are not to be identified she-wise or he-foolishly. Although willing to concede that there may be something formally amiss with constructions of the type *Usually sober, the vicar found him snoring in the vestry*, they argue irrefutably (as they understand that word) that 'the meaning is quite clear'. In general, they have replaced 'correctness' with 'acceptability'. Misspellings do not disturb them, and they seem to regard meanings as negotiable in committee – which, in a broad sense, they indeed are. They have grown up with television, social democracy, and the power of the peer group, and look askance at any authority that will not argue its laws. Only when they are turned out, as wage-earners (or rather, as *salaried employees*), into the world of middle-class institutions and aspirations, do they begin to demand prescriptive rules.

## 5 The diversity of change

Now all this is a ragbag of reflection and anecdote, from which no shaping principle emerges. Yet such scraps of gossip are brief evidences of the powers that create and change usage: of education and attitudes to its purpose; of regional and class dialect; of professions and employments; of the prestige of certain individuals; of fashion, or snobbery, of the need to be socially 'in' and the stress of being 'out'; of imitations, of loyalties, affections, aversions, courtesies; of the fear of innovation and the anxious reverence for old, established things; of the reaction of one generation to another; of the impulse to poeteic creation, humour, figurative language, metaphor. All of which is so diverse, so bewildering in its diversity, so variously printed on our separate lives, that we lose sight of principle and lean heavily on prejudice. This wretched boy calls a *waistcoat* a *vest*; and I cannot *help* noticing *har*ASS for HARass; and I feel that only the semi-observant and the demi-semi-sensitive could have any difficulty at all with non-finite dependent clauses. When we reach the stage of making accusatory comment, we have recognized in ourselves an insecurity that craves authoritarian intervention – by anyone confident enough to tell us, without prevarication, without distracting considerations of 'it all depends', that there is a right position, and that we are in it. What we are really in is the usage trap.

## 6 Criteria of usage and style

The 'right position' presupposes criteria of rightness, and it is just here that longed-for authority begins to veer between the banal and the blindfolded. Expert opinion and hearsay alike endow certain notions with critical status. They are:

(a) *Clarity*
This is said to be achieved by avoiding ambiguity; avoiding 'woolliness' (problem: define 'woolliness'); avoiding 'muddled thinking'; and avoiding unnecessary complexity (but what is 'complex' and what are the limits of 'necessary'?)

(b) *Felicity*
This is achieved by avoiding 'awkwardness'; shunning 'prolixity'; eschewing 'turgidity'; vetting 'vulgarity'; cultivating a fluent continuity.

(c) *Appropriateness*
The secret of this, apparently, is to fit your language to your subject; also to fit your language to your audience; to observe the formalities, or permit the informalities, as the case may be; to use the common tongue commonly and technical terms technically.

(d) *Respect for the status quo*
The essence of this is the belief that all innovation corrupts and must be resisted.

(e) *Repudiation of fashions, mannerisms, and popular models*
Typified by indignant protests such as 'Slang is for people who are too lazy to think,' or 'We are all tired of this trendy jargon,' or 'I don't care if you heard it on TV, read it in the *Guardian*, or heard the Prime Minister say it – *it's wrong*.'

These points are somewhat mischievously framed, in mockery of prescriptions that too often prove to be roundabout, vapouring, and empty – not to say *teapotliddous*. Parody apart, what is represented is a pattern of responses to usage and style, involving three *constructive* tests (i.e. 'Is this clear?', 'Does this read well?', 'Is this the right level of language?') and two *constrictive* reactions ('this innovation worries me'; 'I am annoyed by this trick'). One difficulty that inevitably snares anyone offering counsel on usage is that the constructive becomes the stalking-horse of the constrictive. The latter, ruled by the nose, the nape of the neck, and the nervous system, is beyond the scope of reason and justification. We cannot help our reactions, any more than we can help sneezing and yawning, and we certainly cannot rationalize them. For the constructive, on the other hand, we are required to find supporting arguments; we must say *why* some expression or construction is unclear, infelicitous, or inappropriate, and *how* it may be amended. Possibly a specious activity, this process of justification is nevertheless felt to be sounder than the blank instinctive response of 'This is just wrong, that's all.' So when we find ourselves in a constrictive position, we do our best to shift the fight to constructive ground. I might argue, for example, that the current tendency – virtually an accomplished change – to use the word *refute* as a synonym of *reject* or *deny* offends against the constructive principle of clarity; because by shifting the load of meaning that individual words have to carry, it invites the curse of ambiguity. The argument ostensibly justifies my objection, but it will not survive prolonged investigation. The semantics of English will soon accommodate the shift from *refute* = 'rebut' to *refute* = 'reject', and I will have to accept that my position is constrictive, i.e. that I dislike this usage because I dislike it; because it is a raw upstart; because it upsets what I have learned.

## 7 The elusiveness of criteria

Criteria of usage are difficult to apply effectively and consistently, even when the constructive will is unimpeded by the constrictive reservation. For this there are at least three reasons. One is that we so often make negative recommendations, letting *what should be done* be inferred from indications of *what should not be done*. Clarity, for example, is defined by the injunction to avoid ambiguity, woolliness, or wordiness. (Eric Partridge's *Usage and Abusage* contains the entry CLARITY. The opposite of OBSCURITY, q.v.). Seldom, if at all, is the virtue of clarity expounded positively, through creative exploration of the resources of language; an exploration that asks 'What can be done?', 'Under what circumstances?' and 'How?' A second difficulty is that categories like 'clear', 'felicitous' and 'appropriate' often overlap, or are diverse labels for some vague aesthetic perception. Whatever we like or dislike we mark with approving or disapproving labels: 'clear' or 'unclear' might just as well be 'felicitous' or 'infelicitous', which could without much difference be 'appropriate' or 'inappropriate'. The criteria are really not very distinctive or objective.

A third weakness is that the search for the unclear is a quest that discovers too many phantom blunders and artificial follies. The point is well illustrated by numerous cautionary examples of 'ambiguity' that allow no one to doubt for more than a moment their single intention. This, for example, is not ambiguous:

> It is difficult to be absolutely honest.

Nor is this ambiguous:

> It is difficult, to be absolutely honest.

The two sentences express different meanings, but in neither case is the intended meaning uncertain. Punctuation provides the necessary clue; in speech, this would be done by intonation. It would of course be possible for a writer to convey a meaning *erroneously*, by omitting a comma or by mistakenly inserting one, but that would not be a case of ambiguity. It would be a simple blunder.

Many jokes, howlers, slips of the pen, etc., are said to turn on ambiguities:

> Erected to the memory of James Macmillan, drowned in the Severn by some of his closest friends.

> Prospective employers will be lucky if they get Nottingham graduates to work for them.

Not for a moment are these genuinely ambiguous, if an 'ambiguity' is something that leaves the reader/listener in two minds. Who is so naive as to be puzzled by them? We laugh because we see precisely what is intended, and how the intention has missed its mark (in one case, literally, a mark of punctuation). Such examples might well be cited as casual and amusing *infelicities*, but they are not unclear. In the absence of an explanatory context, this is unclear:

I mean to keep all of father's books in the cabinet downstairs.

Neither a distinctive speech-pattern nor a corrective punctuation can disambiguate this sentence, which suggests two possible patterns of reference, i.e.:

Father owns/owned books. I mean to keep (= store) them all in the cabinet downstairs.

There is a cabinet downstairs. In it are some books that belong/belonged to father. I mean to keep (= retain possession of) them all.

In addition to these conflicts of reference, there are potential differences of *theme* and *focus* (on these terms see 2.7). What is the primary topic of discourse – the books or the cabinet? Various rewritings of the sentence suggest themselves:

I mean to keep all of father's books that are in the cabinet downstairs.

In the cabinet downstairs I mean to keep all of father's books.

All of father's books in the cabinet downstairs I mean to keep.

Of father's books, I mean to keep all that are in the cabinet downstairs.

Spoken English offers other solutions, in the form of utterances that announce a *topic* and append a *comment*, e.g.:

You know father's books? I'm going to keep them all in the cabinet downstairs.

About father's books in the cabinet downstairs. I'm going to keep them all.

The cabinet downstairs – that's where I'm going to keep all of father's books.

This process of topicalization can of course be extended to written English, in the form of such sentences as *With regard* to the books in the cabinet downstairs, I propose to keep them all*, or *As for the cabinet downstairs, I mean to keep all father's books in it.*

### 8 The constructive value of grammar

This example serves to make an important point about the study of grammar. Not that grammar is a panacea for the ills of the verbally inept; not that sentence analysis and the long parsing ever made a stylist; simply that the grammar of a language creates plural resources, offers more than one solution to problems of expression, shows some possibilities, at least, of escaping from the usage trap, which operates on the victim's conviction that there is only *one* answer in each difficult case. It will do nothing to help us if we say *jack* when fashion decrees *knave*, or to enlighten us if we say *invoalve* when prejudice requires *involve*. But if we try to understand the grammar of our language, so as to become sharply aware of the patterns of expression available to us when we speak or write, then we attain something of great constructive value. Grammar can be the workshop, studio, or laboratory of usage. Through it we explore idiom, i.e. we examine the interplay of certain constructions and certain dictionary items; through idiom we test the constraints and allowances of style. Some questions will always elude this grammatical/idiomatic investigation. There is no constructive exploration that will let us come to terms with *serviette* vs *table napkin*, for example, or with *notepaper* vs *writing paper*, or *toilet* vs *lavatory* – because these things are matters of fashion, of regional and temporal variation, of coterie usage, of a trivializing sensitivity to language that has much to do with habit, pretension, self-regard, and almost nothing to do with communication. Usage and style should carry more reliable credentials.

# 2
# A little grammar: Styles of sentences

> What's a' your jargon o' your schools,
> Your Latin names for horns and stools,
> If honest Nature made you fools,
>     What sairs your grammars?
>
> – Robert Burns
>
> Grammere, that grounde is of alle . . .
>
> – William Langland

Since we do need some of the jargon of the schools – enough, at least, to provide constructive references, frames of judgment in stylistic questions – let us examine a few patterns of the English sentence. The patterning may be quite simple:

> Billy stole his father's car

or very complex:

> After the police had scoured three counties, eventually tracing the young culprit to a cinema in Leamington Spa, where he had gone to see a repeat showing of '*Star Wars*', Billy's father was advised that it might be a good idea to keep his son out of mischief by providing the inquisitive little fellow with numerous video games of the sort designed to appeal to the adventurous if potentially felonious instincts of a child growing up in an age of diminishing respect for property.

It is easy to suppose that the first of these two examples might occur in speech, whereas the second could hardly be anything other than a piece of writing. No one, surely, would speak with such elaboration and precision of sentence-design, except perhaps in oratory or prepared – i.e. *scripted* – address.

This does not mean that complex sentences are rare in speech, or that simple structures are foreign to writing. Sentences in spoken English can be quite complex syntactically, as the following, a recorded instance of actual speech, may show:

> While I'm in the village I'll try and see if Mr Ward can find time to pop over later on this afternoon and get those garage doors to hang properly, if that's OK with you.

Many such instances of complex sentence-structure might be noted in ordinary domestic exchanges. It is true, however, that writing, because it relieves us of the burden of memorizing, allows us to produce sentences of greater length and intricacy than those we commonly construct when we speak. The speaker takes his sentences as they come; the writer, on the other hand, plans his text, develops a feeling for gradations of complexity, strives to understand the options relating to styles and functions of the simple and the complex.

## 1 Simple sentences (a): patterns and elements

On p. 17 is a table presenting some patterns of the simple sentence; it specifies certain elements of sentence structure (using a conventional and widely recognized terminology), and provides 'realizations' – i.e. specific instances, concrete examples – of these elements. The distinction between 'element' and 'realization' must be emphasized The names of the elements, e.g. *subject, object, complement*, are abstractions. They do not denote specific words or phrases, or even particular categories of word or phrase. They are the names of functions, or, figuratively speaking, of positions in play. The positions are diversely filled, the functions discharged, or 'realized', in a variety of ways.

The tabulated examples will be seen to unfold a small narrative. The purpose of this is to demonstrate that a text of sorts might be constructed from strictly circumscribed syntactic resources, even though the limitations of such a stylistic enterprise may be readily apparent:

## A little grammar

*Elements of the simple sentence*

| S | V | A | $C_s$ | $O_i$ | $O_d$ | $C_o$ |
|---|---|---|---|---|---|---|
| The lesson | began | | | | | |
| John | wrote | on the blackboard | | | the first example | |
| He | quailed | inwardly | | | | |
| Some of these boys | looked | | so hostile | | | |
| Their undoubted leader | was | | the redheaded lad in the corner | | | |
| The young teacher, a novice in matters of discipline, | could not face | | | | that insolent stare | |
| He | gave | | | the others | a timid smile | |
| Those hardbitten veterans of classroom wars | must have considered | | | | him | a simpering idiot |

The elements of simple sentency-structure are:

    S  = Subject
    V  = Verb
    $O_d$ = Direct Object
    $O_i$ = Indirect Object
    $C_s$ = Subject Complement
    $C_o$ = Object Complement
    A  = Adverbial

The terminology is that used in *A Grammar of Contemporary English*, by Randolph Quirk, Sidney Greenbaum, Geoffrey Leech and Jan Svartvik

The lesson began. John wrote on the blackboard the first example. He quailed inwardly. Some of these boys looked so hostile. Their undoubted ringleader was the red-headed lad in the corner. The young teacher, a novice in matters of discipline, could not face that insolent stare. He gave the others a timid smile. Those hard-bitten veterans of class-room wars must have considered him a simpering idiot.

Each step in the story is a simple *declarative* sentence (i.e. a sentence making a statement) with a pattern requiring basically S and V, as obligatory elements. At S, as at O and C, occur so-called *nominal* items, i.e. nouns or noun-related expressions. Here are some of the nominal items realizing the element S in the sentences that unfold the tale of John's classroom ordeal:

a personal name, or *proper noun* (*John*)

a general name, or *common noun* (*the lesson*)

a *noun phrase*, i.e. a group of words with a noun as its *head* or indispensable member (*those hard-bitten* VETERANS)

a pair of noun phrases *in apposition*, i.e. as *tandem partners* (*the young teacher + a novice in matters of discipline*)

a *personal pronoun* (*he*)

These typify the general rule that in simple sentences S is realized by nouns, noun phrases, or pronouns. The noun phrase in its turn has simple and complex realizations. Simple instances are *a teacher*, *the class*; complex, *a very badly behaved senior school class*, *the incorrigible hooligans' long-suffering young English teacher*, *that first disastrous, never-to-be-forgotten General Certificate class with those hooligans in the fifth form school-leaving set*. In complex noun phrases, the *head* is augmented by an array of *modifiers*, which may precede it or follow it. In these examples, the word WINE is the head of the noun phrase:

not at all unpalatable Californian WINE
WINE in large bottles with colourful labels

Such patterns are called, respectively, *premodification* and *postmodification*. In phrases of highly complex structure, the head may be pre- and postmodified:

not at all unpalatable Californian WINE in large bottles with colourful labels

Rules of sequence govern the ordering of modifying items. There is, furthermore, some correlation between the type of modification and the character of the information conveyed; e.g., in the following, between premodification and 'permanent characteristic', postmodification and 'temporary characteristics':

that one-legged Spanish RUFFIAN with his arm round Auntie

Other examples, however, simply suggest the value of pre- and postmodification as stylistic alternatives. We may write, for example, *an idiotically grinning police sergeant*, or, with a slight modification of wording, *a police sergeant with an idiotic grin*. In such cases there is an apparent choice, which must be related to the demands of a wider context. The choice is not always available. We may convert, or 'transpose', the premodified *ruffian with a wooden leg* into *wooden-legged ruffian*; but we cannot as convincingly transpose *ruffian with a horrible green eye-patch* – though *horribly green eye-patched ruffian* might be considered a striking turn of literary style. The normal prohibitions of usage sometimes challenge the creative spirit.

Some intricate notions and orientations to reality are expressed by realizations of the element V. These are not copiously exemplified in the narrative of John and his class, but a few pages of any novel or work of expository prose would certainly demand a reader's competence to recognize and 'decode' the following:

(1) The notion of time, grammatically represented in *tense* (e.g. the past tense forms of *began, wrote, quailed*).

(2) Notions of possibility, preference, choice, permission, necessity, contingency, etc., expressed in *mood*; e.g. 'they *must have considered* him a simpering idiot', where *must* expresses a conjecture on the part of the protagonist in the narrative.

(3) Notions of perspective, or 'slant', on the event-in-time; called, in grammar, *aspect*. English regularly makes two important aspectual distinctions, in connection with expressions of tense. We distinguish between the completed event (*Noah built the ark one afternoon, before it rained*), and the event in duration, or in progressive overlap with other events (*Noah was building the ark one afternoon when it came on to rain*). We make another kind of aspectual distinction in reference to past events, which may be reported in the simple past (e.g. *I worked in London*), or in the past with the so-called 'perfective' aspect (e.g. *I have lived in London*). Expressions of past time may thus involve, variously, the simple past (*I read your book*), the past + progressive aspect (*I was reading your book*), past + perfective aspect (*I have read your book*), past + progressive + perfective aspects (*I have been reading your book*).

These complex and interlinking notions are conveyed in the *verb phrase*, which in its simplest form consists of the bare *lexical verb*, the word denoting an activity, a process, an event, a relation, etc. In a more complex form of verb phrase, the lexical verb is the head which is preceded by a sequence of *auxiliaries*. Some of the latter express mood, and are hence called *modal* (*can, could, may, might, shall, will, should, would, must, ought to, need, dare*). Other auxiliaries (e.g. *have, be, do*) help to specify tense and aspect (*We have been here before, He is taking his morning walk*), or in speech convey the emphasis of corrections and affirmations (e.g. *I have checked, it is ready, we did try,* in response to *you should have checked, I thought it would be ready, why didn't you try?*)

## 2 Simple sentences (b): complementation

Many simple sentences are constructed on the basic pattern SV:

The lesson began.
John trembled.

# A little grammar

The lesson on the structure of noun phrases in English began.
John must have been trembling.
The lady in the green frock has arrived.
That one-legged Spanish ruffian with the horrible green eye-patch is snoring.

It is common, however, for the stem-structure, SV, to be extended in some way, for example through the addition of an adverbial element, A. Some examples of the SVA pattern (the diagonals mark out the three elements):

Our luggage/ has arrived/ at last.
The man in the next room/ has been snoring/ all night.
We/ are leaving/ on Friday.
The Thompsons/ are leaving/ now.
They/ have suffered/ here.
The manager/ behaves/ dreadfully.
The food/ comes/ in dirty little plastic containers.
The washbasin/ fell/ on Mr Thompson's foot.
Mrs Thompson/ cries/ a lot.

The A element may be a single adverb of time (*now*), place (*here*), or manner (*dreadfully*), or an adverbial phrase (*at last, all night, a lot*), or a prepositional phrase, i.e. a noun phrase introduced by a preposition (*on Friday, in dirty little plastic containers, on Mr Thompson's foot*).

In other patterns, the SV base is *complemented* by a C or an O. In the pattern SVC, a verb of the type *be, become, look, seem*, is followed by a *subject complement*, an adjective or nominal item related to or equated with the subject of the sentence; e.g. *comic, a neglected genius* in

The first murderer looked comic.
Van Gogh was a neglected genius.

This kind of complementation is sometimes called *intensive*, as opposed to the *extensive* complementation of the SVO pattern. Compare

The first murderer looked comic (SVC intensive)

with

The audience loved the first murderer (SVO extensivē)

or

Van Gogh was a neglected genius (SVC intensive)

with

His contemporaries neglected the genius of Van Gogh (SVO extensive)

The arrows indicate the structural relationships of 'intending' and 'ex-tending'. In the last example, the phrase *the genius of Van Gogh* realizes a *direct object*, an element which, like S, is represented in the simple sentence by nominal items.

The primary structures SVA, SVC, SVO are compounded in more elaborate patterns:

Shakespeare / left / his second-best bed / to his wife. (SVOA)
The Thompsons / were / miserable / all week. (SVCA)

SVO may combine with an element $O_i$, *indirect object*, or with $C_o$, *object complement*:

Shakespeare / left / his wife / his second-best bed. (SVO$_i$O)
She / found / the mattress / lumpy. (SVO$_d$ C$_o$)

These extended structures admit of further extension through the addition of an A element:

Mr Thompson / gave / the manager / a piece of his mind / next morning. (SVO$_i$ O$_d$ A)

A more enlightened age / would have made / Van Gogh / comfortable / with a pension. (SVOC$_o$ A)

### 3 Transitivity

Verbs in the pattern SVO, which take *extensive* complementation, are classified as *transitive*. (*Transitive*, like *extensive*, carries its purport in its etymology; it signifies, literally, 'going across', i.e. from its point of departure in the SV group to its goal in the O) The pattern SVO$_i$O (as in *I must send my publisher a note of apology*) is by some grammarians called *distransitive*, there being two 'goals', the indirect object (*my publisher*) and the direct object (*a note of apology*). Verbs in the pattern of *intensive* complementation, SVC or that of adverbial extension, SVA, or the bare stem-formula, SV, are said to be *intransitive*. In fact, transitivity and intransitivity are not so much properties of the verb itself as of the patterns into which the verb enters. Some verbs are regularly intransitive, e.g. *arrive, expire* (thus *We went to the station to see if Daddy had arrived; while we were away the tortoise expired;* not *We went to the station to see if we could arrive Daddy; while we were away some scoundrel expired the tortoise*). Some verbs, e.g. *weep, sigh, laugh, wink*, are essentially intransitive, but may occasionally figure transitively, with a direct object in the form of a correspondent or semantically equivalent noun (e.g. *she sighed a deep sigh; the giant winked a gargantuan wink; the tyrant laughs his laugh; the oppressed weep their tears*).

In numerous instances a verb will enter into both transitive and intransitive patterns. Thus, *smoke*:

    Jack / smokes                          (SV intransitive)

or

    Jack / smokes/ too much           (SVA intransitive)

but

    Jack / smokes / too many cigarettes.    (SVO transitive)

Another example, *ponder*:

    The Faculty Board / pondered         (SV intransitive)

    The Faculty Board / pondered / for three and a half hours.
                                           (SVA intransitive)

    The Faculty Board / pondered / the wording of a paragraph.
                                            (SVO transitive)

The meaning of a verb may be determined by its patterning; e.g. *reflect*, in *Mary sat and reflected for a few moments*, is intransitive and is synonymous with *think*, but in *Her spectacles reflected the evening sunlight* it is transitive, and has the sense of 'throw back'.

## 4 Stative and dynamic

English verbs are variously compatible with the progressive aspect. Verbs denoting activities or processes will as a rule take the progressive, whereas some types, e.g. cognitive verbs like *believe, perceive, recognize*, ordinarily resist it. It is thus good English to say *I was ardently embracing Mrs Fothergill*, but unidiomatic to add *when suddenly I was perceiving the barrel of her husband's shotgun*. We distinguish semantically between *dynamic* and *stative* verbs. In their grammar, dynamic verbs like *work, run, argue*, accept the progressive forms (*he worked – he was working*, etc.); stative verbs like *be, know, consist*, do not. This generally convenient distinction is often blurred, as some verbs change their category with their context. For instance, we take it as a rule that *know* is stative and therefore not amenable to the progressive aspect: *She is knowing a good psychiatrist* and *I have been knowing this city for twenty years* are considered incorrect. But in certain cases, e.g. in hypothetical statements about future events, *know* can assume the dynamic/progressive character: *We should be knowing the results in a few days' time* (= *We should be learning the results, We should be getting to know the results*).

## 5 Order of elements in the simple sentence

For purposes of illustration, and because it effectively represents the 'normal' syntactic order, it is convenient to regard the simple declarative sentence as beginning with the elements SV. In fact, observation of everyday usage will remind us that this is a rule with frequent exceptions, and that S may be preceded by A, or even by C or O:

Really funny it was. (CSV)
A right Charlie I felt. (CSV)
Snobs I can't stand. (OSV)
Foreman, they made him. ($C_o$ SVO)
Twenty pages of notes I gave that half-wit. ($O_d$ $SVO_i$)

Apparently there is some latitude in the ordering of sentence elements, a freedom that has a stylistic value. Consider the example:

His friends he cherished; his enemies he gave no respite.

What is immediately apparent about this is that it marks with quite powerful emphasis the formulation of something that might have been expressed in less rhetorical terms, as *He cherished his friends; he gave no respite to his enemies.* Indeed, the *fronting*, as we call it, of O or C invariably produces a sense of the *marked* construction, emphatically deviant from the customary, or *unmarked* pattern.

Some examples of 'normal' sentence structures, side by side with the same sentences marked by fronting:

Bill would drink cup after cup of tea. (SVO)
Cup after cup of tea Bill would drink. (OSV)

The postman brings some of our mail after lunch. (SVOA)
Some of our mail the postman brings after lunch. (OSVA)

They gave Tom a second chance. ($SVO_i\ O_d$)
Tom they gave a second chance. ($O_i\ SVO_d$)

Hamlet was a melancholy fellow. (SVC)
A melancholy fellow Hamlet was. (CSV)
A melancholy fellow was Hamlet. (CVS)

They made that rascal Professor of Ethics. ($SVOC_o$)
Professor of Ethics they made that rascal. ($C_o\ SVO$)
That rascal they made Professor of Ethics. ($OSVC_o$)

### 6 Location of adverbials

The location of adverbials in the simple sentence pattern is often a matter of stylistic interest, and sometimes creates problems of usage. They commonly occur at the end of the sentence:

The Professor of Comparative Anthropology wears lipstick on Fridays. (SVOA)

The Dean of Agriculture looks heavenly in fish-net tights. (SVCA)

Even when there is more than one adverbial, the end-position is common:

The Reader in Necromancy will conduct his seminar in the Senior Common Room at two-thirty (SVOAA)

A lecturer in Ergonomics fell heavily down the stairs twenty minutes ago. (SVOAAA)

Members of the Senate convene for dubious purposes in the Board Room on the first Wednesday of every month at two-fifteen punctually. (SVAAAAA)

The types of adverbial illustrated here are called *manner* (Am – a somewhat unsatisfactory name for a rather broad semantic category), *place*, (Ap) and *time* (At). Am, Ap, At is the sequence in which they commonly occur:

The Research Fellow in Geriatrics worked happily in this room for forty years. (SVAmApAt)

She went dutifully to the library every day. (SVAmApAt)

The 'rule' of manner-place-time is by no means a stylistic commandment. The number of adverbials involved, the type of realization (as word or phrase) and the influence of particular items of vocabulary, to say nothing of questions of contextual emphasis, all create that fruitful uncertainty which is the making of style and usage. Which, we may ask, is stylistically preferable, the sentence *The professor stormed in a mood of prophetic rage down the corridor at half past ten*, or *The professor stormed down the corridor at half past ten in a mood of prophetic rage*? The first has the order SVAmApAt, while the second, which may be thought to give the better reading, is sequenced SVApAtAm. One motive for preferring the latter sequence could be the perception that *down* is dually related, to the verb it follows (compare *The professor came storming down on us*), and to the phrase it introduces (*down the corridor*), and consequently that this Ap ought to come next to the verb. A further reason might be that the phrase *in a mood of prophetic rage*, being longer than *down the corridor* and *at half past ten*, creates a cadence, a rhythmic weighting.

A third factor is *focus*, i.e. the placing of emphasis on important information.

## 7 Focus

In simple sentences, information is customarily processed with a movement from 'known' to 'unknown', or 'given' to 'new', or 'topic' to 'comment':

Our butcher has run away with a vegetarian.

Here the subject of the sentence, *Our butcher*, provides the 'given' information, or 'topic' ('I say, you know our butcher?') while the predicate furnishes an amplifying 'comment' ('well, he's run away with a vegetarian') comprising 'new' information answering questions of matter ('what?') and manner ('how?' 'Under what circumstances?' 'With whom?')

The inital element of such sentences, expounding 'given' information or a proposed 'topic', is sometimes called the *theme*. A companion term, *focus*, relates to the word or phrase that carries the main, commentary burden of 'new' information, e.g. the word *vegetarian* in our example; in speech the focus is accentually marked, e.g.:

Aunt Mary's wolfhound bit the young *post*man.
(focus on *postman*)

Aunt Mary's wolfhound bit the *young* postman.
(focus on *young* = as opposed to the older postman / other postmen)

Aunt Mary's wolfhound *bit* the young postman.
(corrective focus on *bit*, e.g. not *licked*)

The first of these examples has the *end-focus* that characterizes unmarked forms of the simple declarative sentence.

Clearly, the ordering of elements in a sentence can affect the theme-focus relationship. When, for example,

He's run away with a vegetarian

becomes

A vegetarian he's run away with!
(= 'of all things!' 'what d'you think of *that*?')

the fronting creates a focus-bearing theme, or *marked theme*. It is thus possible for a sentence to be doubly focused:

> Every blessed day he feeds those confounded pigeons.

Here the emphatic marking of a theme accompanies a no less emphatic end-focus.

## 8 The passive as focusing device

Fronting is one way of adjusting the informational focus. Another is to convert active into passive. Thus

> (1) Jack fed the hungry birds

may be recast in the form

> (2) The hungry birds were fed by Jack.

In example (1) the subject-element is realized by the name of an *agent*, Jack; the object-element by a noun denoting *recipients*, the birds; and the sentence is focused on the noun indicating the recipient role. In example (2) the subject-element is realized by the noun phrase denoting the role of recipient; an adverbial phrase (*by Jack*) indicates the agent-role; and the focus is now on the word naming an agent (*Jack*). The passive transformation refocuses the sentence.

Note that the agentive 'by-phrase' is often omitted, i.e. if the identity of the agent is irrelevant, or unknown, or, possibly, if there is more than one agent. This is not uncommon in narrative. We may tell a simple tale in the active voice:

> Jean has washed the dishes, Joan has put the children to bed, Jack has made up the fire.

Or in the passive:

> The dishes have been washed by Jean, the children have been put to bed by Joan, the fire has been made up by Jack.

But if we wish to present a tale of *events* rather than to focus on personalities, we omit the by-phrases:

> The dishes have been washed, the children have been put to bed, the fire has been made up.

A further step in this instance might well be to delete the auxiliary verbs from the first and second clauses:

> The dishes have been washed, the children put to bed, the fire made up.

### 9 Postpositioning

Some special sentence-forms facilitate the postponement of items into a position of end-focus. One of these is the so-called *existential* sentence, exemplified by the assertion *There is a reason*, in which a 'dummy' subject *there* is followed by the verb *be*, which in its turn is followed by the 'true' subject, *a reason*. If the statement were cast in the form *A reason exists*, end-focus would bring the verb, *exists*, into prominence, whereas the existential construction focuses on *a reason*.

The general formula for the existential sentence is:

> There + BE + S + (phrase or clause)
>        or other
>        existential
>        verb, e.g.
>        'exist'
>        'occur'
>        'come'

Some examples:

> There is a God.
> There was someone at the door.
> There may be no reason to suspect him.
> There then occurred a remarkable event.

Existential sentences thus offer alternative formulations to simple sentences (e.g. *A remarkable event occurred* vs *There occurred a remarkable event*). In a few cases, the existential construction is the standard form. Thus, we usually assert the existence of a supreme being with the sentence *There is a God*. We might say *God exists*, or *God is*, but these formulations – particularly the latter – put a stark focus on the verb.

Another 'postpositioning' structure is the *extraposition*, patterned as follows:

IT + BE + C + (clause)
          seem
          appear
          happen
          etc.

Examples:

  It was a pity (that) you could not come.
  It seemed heartless to wake her.
  It appears (likely) that he has broken his leg.

The clause following C is the 'true' grammatical subject of the sentence, shifted into a position where it takes end-focus. The first two examples can be rewritten so that this clause becomes the first element, or theme: *That you could not come was a pity*, *To wake her seemed heartless*. The third example can only be re-written in this way if a complement (e.g. *likely*, *true*, *probable*) is supplied: *That he has broken his leg appears likely*. In this, as in the other rewritings, the complement is now the element that takes end-focus.

The *cleft sentence* has a superficial resemblance to the extraposition. From a single clause, e.g. *The dog ate my dinner*, we may derive twin-clause forms (hence 'cleft'), such as *It was the dog that ate my dinner*, or *It was my dinner (that) the dog ate*. The formula for the cleft sentence is:

IT + BE + S/C/A/O + who/that-clause

the focus is on the element immediately following BE; it is thus possible to compose cleft sentences clearly indicative of a focus on subject, object, complement, or adverbial. Some examples:

  It was Darwin who developed the theory of evolution.
  (= 'Darwin developed the theory of evolution'; focus on S)

  It was my money (that) you lost.
  (= 'You lost my money'; focus on O).

  It was here that the battle was fought.
  (= 'The battle was fought here'; focus on A)

  It was green that we painted the bathroom.
  (= 'We painted the bathroom green'; focus on Co)

## A little grammar

The cleft sentence is a formula of some stylistic value, enabling the writer to demonstrate a special or contrastive focus without having to resort to the typographical shifts of underlining, bold type, capitals, etc.

The *pseudo-cleft* sentence is an SVC pattern in which S or C is realized by a wh-clause (most often *what*, sometimes *who*, *which*, *why*, *how*), e.g.;

> What mother painted last year was the bathroom.
> Why she did it is a mystery.
> How she managed is a miracle.
> A medal is what she deserves.
> What she did was paint the whole place brown.

In current colloquial English, a sense of syntactic cleavage in sentences like the last-quoted often prompts the restoration of a deleted subject to the clause realizing C:

> What mother did was, she painted the bathroom.
> What we're going to do now is, we're going to put this card into this little bag.

In such structures, one clause (the wh-clause) appears as 'topic', the other as 'comment'.

### 10 Structural variation and focus-shift

Many shifts of focus become possible when frontings, passive transformations, and 'postpositioning' structures are taken into account. Here are some variations on a sentence:

> Father painted the wall deep purple.
> Deep purple, father painted that wall.
> Deep purple was what father painted the wall.
> What father painted the wall was deep purple.
> What father did was paint the wall deep purple.
> What he did was, he painted it deep purple.
> The wall was painted deep purple by father.
> That particular wall father painted deep purple.
> There was a wall that father painted deep purple.
> There was one wall that was painted deep purple by father.
> There was this wall – deep purple, father painted it.

That wall there – painted it deep purple, father did.
It's a fact that father painted the wall deep purple.
It was father who painted the wall deep purple.
It was deep purple that father painted the wall.

Such elementary demonstrations point to the existence of a wide grammatical *repertoire*; a simple declaration may be made in many ways, with diverse emphases, with varied contextual implications, with gradations of appropriateness to speech or writing.

## 11 Complexity

Many of the examples in the last two sections fall into the category of *complex* sentences. They embody more than one clause, i.e. more than one process of the type represented by SV, SVA, SVC, SVO, etc. In the following sentence, for example, one clause is embedded in another:

What mother painted last year was the bathroom.

The simple sentence *Mother painted it last year* (SVOA) becomes an embedded clause realizing the element S in a complex sentence, the structure of which may be represented as follows:

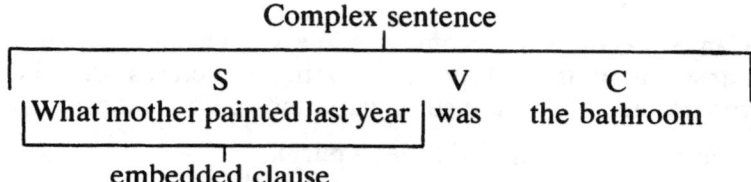

A complex sentence, then, in some way elaborates or reduplicates the SV etc. process, whether by embedding, as in the example above, or by some other mode of interlinking. Most of the sentences we use in writing or in continuous speech are complex. Earlier in this chapter we tried to compose a piece of narrative in simple sentences. It would be difficult to do this at any great length, and in some types of discourse, e.g. the conduct of argument, it would be virtually impossible. There is a recurrent need to expound facts or

## A little grammar

concepts in greater elaboration than the structure of the simple sentence permits. Consider, for example, the expressions of time in the following:

(1) She will come later.
(2) She will come whenever she can manage to get rid of her visitors.

Here we have a simple and a complex sentence, each conveying the message 'She will come at some time'. In the simple sentence, the notion 'some time' is embodied in the adverb *later*. In the complex sentence 'some time' is expressed by a *subordinate clause* (*whenever she can manage to get rid of her visitors*), in which a *non-finite clause* (*to get rid of her visitors*) is embedded. The simple and general notion *later* is elaborated in this complex structure.

In speech as well as in writing there is an incessant need to supplement, modify, and elucidate, clarifying questions of time, identity, reason, result, process, instrumentality, etc. These motivations make for grammatical complexity. Furthermore, the complex sentence expresses the close linkage – the contingency, causality, or simultaneity – of ideas, circumstances, and events. Two simple sentences taken conjointly (e.g. *I ate the cake. I was hungry* may suggest a causal relationship, but do not expound the contingency of action and explanation as patently as a complex structure incorporating the two statements (e.g. *I ate the cake because I was hungry, Being hungry I ate the cake, I was hungry so I ate the cake*, etc). Simple sentences present simple sequences: *He opened the door. He faced his accusers*; *She washed the dishes. She found a gold filling.* Complex sentences can convey a sense of overlapping events, or of co-occurrences: *Opening the door, he faced his accusers; While washing the dishes, she found a gold filling.* In these and in other ways the complex sentences express modes of perception and cognition.

### 12 Coordination

Simple sentence units enter into the complex sentence as clauses, the linkage of which is frequently indicated by *conjunctions*. One very common conjunction is the word *and* which can be used to *coordinate* so-called *independent* clauses:

We went on foot over the fields (Independent clause)

and (Coordinator)

the children travelled by car. (Independent clause)

The coordinator makes a non-dependent relationship between simple sentences which thus form the clauses of a higher unit, the complex sentence *We went on foot over the fields and the children travelled by car*. Neither of the clauses in this example has priority of meaning over the other; we could easily reverse their order – *The children travelled by car and we went on foot over the fields* – without damaging the sense of the sentence. The same would be generally true of sentences constructed with *but* and *or*, which are also coordinating conjunctions:

The children wanted a picnic, but the adults voted for bridge

or

The adults voted for bridge, but the children wanted a picnic

and

We could fry some eggs or we could go to a restaurant

or

We could go to a restaurant or we could fry some eggs.

Consider, however, some further examples:

We went on foot and the children followed by car next day.

The children wanted a picnic, but Janice had one of her famous headaches.

Here the order of the clauses is perhaps not so obviously or so freely reversible; turning the sentence around may imply a shift of meaning:

We went on foot and the children followed by car next day
(= parties travel on sequent days)

is not necessarily the same as

> The children followed by car next day, and we went on foot (possibly = both parties are 'followers', travelling on the same day; i.e. 'the children travelled by car while we went on foot')

and

> The children wanted a picnic but Janice had one of her famous headaches
> (= therefore no picnic)

is not clearly paraphrased by

> Janice had one of her famous headaches but the children wanted a picnic.

(possibly = 'nevertheless we went ahead with the picnic')

These examples point to the possibility of a variable semantic dependence between so-called 'independent' units. The specific wording of the component clauses is clearly of importance (e.g. *followed* and *next day* imply a sequence), and it appears that a coordinating conjunction is not an 'empty' sign of grammatical linkage, but may imply various meanings (e.g. *but* = 'on the other hand', *but* = 'with a constraint, limitation, or reservation', and *but* = 'despite which, overridingly').

It depends, of course, what we mean by *independent*. Confusion is avoided if the term is regarded purely in a grammatical sense. In the sentence *The children wanted an outing, but Janice had one of her famous headaches* there is a semantic relationship between clauses which are nevertheless called 'independent' because neither bears any structural mark of subordination or incompletion. The conjunction *but* makes a grammatical link, but it is a link standing *outside* and *between* the two clauses.

## 13 Subordination

Another way of linking clauses in complex structures is called *subordination*. In the following sentences, the word *although* functions as a subordinator:

> (1) I liked the thesis, although Peter had reservations.

(2) Although I liked the thesis, Peter had reservations.
(3) Although Peter had reservations, I liked the thesis.
(4) Peter had reservations, although I liked the thesis.

In each example there is a *principal* or *main clause* (In examples 1 and 3, *I liked the thesis*, in 2 and 4, *Peter had reservations*), and a *dependent* or *subordinate* clause integrally marked by its subordinating conjunction (*although*). In these examples the clauses are freely reversible, i.e. can occur in the order main-subordinate or subordinate-main, but the subordinating conjunction always remains a part of the dependent clause, marking its subordinate role, and is never construed as a link standing outside clause-structure. The subordinate clause therefore has the form of an incomplete utterance, because the incorporated conjunction implies that there is something left to be said: *Although I liked the thesis . . .*; *Because Janice had a headache . . .*; *When he comes . . .*; *Since you do not reply . . .* etc.

Not all subordinating relationships are expressed by conjunctions. In many sentences the subordinate clause is *nonfinite*:

Driving to Savannah, we laughed a good deal.
(Compare 'As we drove to Savannah we laughed a good deal.')

I would give a lot to see Charleston again.
(Compare 'I would give a lot if I could see Charleston again.')

He worked on desperately, shunned by his colleagues.
(Compare 'While he worked on desperately, his colleagues shunned him.')

*Driving to Savannah* and *shunned by his colleagues* are *participle clauses*, i.e. clauses in which V is realized by the present or past participle of a verb. *To see Charleston again* is an *infinitive clause*; V is realized by the infinitive form of the verb.

Some subordinate clauses are verbless:

Sprightly as ever, he cycled across the Sahara at the ripe old age of seventy-two.

They found his lordship under the table, dead to the world.

In these examples, *sprightly as ever* and *dead to the world* can be construed as verbless clauses having an *adjectival* relationship to the main clause. They may be compared with non-finite clauses like *to tell the truth* or *given the circumstances*, which qualify the main clause *adverbially*. Compare

> Plucky as ever, he ran well
> (*Plucky* etc. relates adjectivally to *he*)

with

> Given the circumstances, he ran well
> (*Given* etc. comments adverbially on *ran well*)

Expressions like *given the circumstances* are in effect *disjuncts*, items making a comment, a reservation, a qualification of some sort. Typical disjuncts are *amazingly, actually, oddly enough, naturally, of course*:

> Amazingly, he cycled across the Sahara at the age of seventy-two.
> They found his lordship under the table, actually.
> My wallet was handed in, oddly enough.
> Naturally, the cash was missing.
> I had reported the theft, of course.

Note that disjuncts are not integrated with the clauses whose meaning they qualify. We might compare *amazingly* as adverb, in *He cycled amazingly across the Sahara* (= 'in an amazing manner'), with *amazingly* as disjunct, in *Amazingly, he cycled across the Sahara* (= 'I am amazed by this'). (On *hopefully, thankfully* as disjuncts and adverbs, see p.152.) Disjunctive expressions are commonly single words or short phrases, but may also take the form of a clause with fixed wording:

> Believe it or not, he cycled across the Sahara at the age of seventy two.
>
> They found his lordship under the table, to tell the truth.
>
> My wallet was handed in, strange to say.
>
> As expected, the cash was missing.
>
> I had reported the theft, needless to add.

## 14 Branching

There are two major ways in which subordinate clauses may be structurally related to a principal construction. One relationship is sequential: in the left-to-right progression of the text, the dependent material either precedes or follows the main clause, e.g.:

(1) Although he had come very early, in the compulsive way of one who frets about punctuality and consults his watch every minute, he almost missed the interview.

(2) He almost missed the interview, although he was one of those people who go very early to any appointment, consulting their watches every minute, so fretful are they about punctuality.

The arrangement in example 1, where the principal clause (*he almost missed the interview*) is placed at the end, or 'right' of the text, is called *left-branching*; example 2 illustrates the converse strategy of *right-branching*. These are important possibilities in the repertoire of stylistic choice. For example, left-branching is frequently used to hold attention, create suspense, or delay the giving of information, while right-branching often occurs in contexts which require the establishment of fact or principle before the making of qualifying comment. A further possibility is *mid-branching*:

(3) He almost – despite his early arrival, his compulsive fretting about punctuality, and his habit of consulting his watch every minute – missed the interview.

Here the elaborate parenthesis is a literary device that serves to sharpen focus on *almost* and *missed the interview*. The example might suggest the casually interruptive habit of speech (*He almost – would you believe it – missed the interview*), but such sentences are as a rule deliberately designed, for writing or for oratory.

## 15 Embedding

A second possibility is *embedding*; the subordinate clause is incorporated into the structure of the principal clause, as in the sentence *What mother painted last year was the bathroom* (see p.32). In that sentence, the clause *What mother painted last year* is embedded, as the realization of the element S, in the structure of a superordinate clause. Two further examples, with non-finite clauses as S:

To save money / can be / hard. (SVC)
Starting the car / proved / difficult. (SVC)

An embedded clause may function as Object:

Everyone / could see / what had been done (SVO)

or as Indirect Object:

He / gave / whoever was in charge / a piece of his mind ($SVO_i\ O_d$)

or as Subject Complement:

Security / is / what most people desire (SVC)

or as Object Complement:

Suffering / has made / him / what he is (SVOC)

or as Adverbial:

My belongings / lay / where I had left them (SVA)

Non-finite clauses have potentially ambiguous relationships with the main clause. Punctuation (or in speech the intonation pattern) signals the distinction between linear (branching) and embedded constructions. Compare

We didn't ask them, to tell the truth
(*to tell the truth* comments disjunctively on the statement *We didn't ask them*; compare *We didn't ask them, actually*)

with

We didn't ask them to tell the truth
(*to tell the truth* is embedded, as O, in a superordinate clause; compare *We didn't ask them that*)

and compare

He stopped, puffing at his cigarette
(a right-branching relationship of principal and subordinate clause)

with

He stopped puffing at his cigarette
(the non-finite clause is embedded; compare *He stopped work*).

## 16 Beyond the sentence

Grammatical relationships continue beyond the confines of the sentence, entering into the larger structure of the text or extended utterance, in such a way that the *cohesion* of the elaborated pattern is continually demonstrated. This is a topic of such breadth as to defy treatment in a few pages, and the following passage will serve only for purposes of brief general illustration:

> It has been suggested that grammatical change can best be interpreted in terms of the community of speech rather than in terms of the psychology and physiology of the individual. If this is indeed so, it might then appear that the examples of grammatical change so far given challenge this principle, since phenomena like analogy and levelling are amenable to psychological rather than social explanations. We must consider, however, that the border between individual psychology and communal tendency is necessarily ill-defined; and also that there is nothing that passes into the communal domain that does so without meeting resistance and censorship. All linguistic change tends to be communally suspect as 'corruption' or 'innovation'; so much so, that any modification would probably be rejected were it not for the fact that changes in their onset are covert, devious, departing from accepted norms by margins too trivial to be observed. Furthermore, there are times when 'accepted norms' are not available. Writing, for example, tends to create a set of grammatical norms; if letters and literacy are not a general characteristic of a culture, or if for some reason the literate tradition is interrupted, the likelihood of accelerated grammatical change is increased. Institutions provide us with another

kind of norm. At first sight, it may seem extravagant to claim that our concepts of public behaviour and of personal relationships in various contexts can have an effect on our grammatical system, but the case is not difficult to make.
(Walter Nash, *Our Experience of Language*)

This paragraph from a textbook on language unfolds its argument by means of small features of wording that connect one sentence with another and integrate the whole passage into a larger context. Any reader encountering the passage in isolation, as it appears here, can readily infer the existence of a preceding and a subsequent text. *So far given* indicates that something has gone before, and *at first sight* suggests that something is to follow. Such expressions reveal that the text is not complete in itself; otherwise, it stands as a self-sustaining unit, by virtue of diverse linkages that connect and group its successive statements.

Consider, for example, the relationship of the first two sentences. The first sentence ends with the long extraposed clause *that grammatical change can best be interpreted in terms of the community of speech rather than in terms of the psychology and physiology of the individual*. (On extraposition see p.30.) In the second sentence, the word *this* is used *anaphorically*, in backward reference, making a link with that long clause: *this = that grammatical change can best be interpreted*, etc. If we note how the linkage is reinforced by *indeed*, which makes a connection with *suggested*, it becomes apparent that an expository strand of syntax runs through the first two sentences: *it has been suggested . . . if indeed this . . . then (that)*. This process extends into the third sentence, where the linking item is the conjunct *however*, taking into scope the preceding *it might (then) appear*.

The first three sentences are held together in the structure designated by *it has been suggested . . . if indeed this . . . then (that) . . . however (the following)*. Between the third and fourth sentences there is a break in syntactic linkage; a new process of framing begins with *All linguistic change tends to be communally suspect as 'corruption' or 'innovation'*. This topic-asserting clause is linked to its successor (after the semi-colon) by the phrase *so much so* (= 'this is emphatically the case', 'the foregoing is true to the extent that . . .'). In the next sentence the linking expression is *furthermore*, reinforcing an assertion by adducing an additional circumstance; and in the sixth sentence it is the phrase *for example* that makes the link. Another syntactic frame has now been constructed: *All linguistic change tends to be communally suspect . . . so much so (that) . . . furthermore . . . for example*. The sentence *Institutions provide us with another kind of norm* starts a new grouping, even though its vocabulary is linked with that sort of preceding sentence: *another kind of norm* recalls *a set of grammatical norms*. The final sentence, beginning *at first sight*, starts the process of framing the next phase in the argument; we anticipate a link of some sort, and in fact the first sentence of the next paragraph contains the phrase *for example*, in backward reference to *the case is not difficult to make*.

Only a few of the devices used to link sentences in continuous discourse are represented here. There is an elaborate repertoire of words and phrases that effect coordinations, subordinations, emphases, antitheses, corrections, disjunctions, etc., in the extended text. Such items add a further range of options – text-framing options – to those involved in the making of sentences, and are an important stage in the progress that leads from the simplest facts of grammar to the most complicated possibilities of style.

### 17 The grammatical repertoire

Grammar regularly offers more than one way of making a statement, marking an emphasis, putting a point, or achieving any expressive aim. There are, in effect, syntactic synonyms, comparable with the synonyms of vocabulary in that no two equivalents make an exact match of meaning. For example, the sentence *I wrote the book easily* can be reformulated in a variety of syntactic shapes:

> To write the book was easy.
> The book was easy to write.
> It was easy to write the book.
> Writing the book was easy.
> The writing of the book was easy.
> The book was easily written.

Only by locating each of these in a context might we judge its appropriateness. Just as words may be deemed 'synonymous' but not co-terminous, so forms of sentences – e.g. *The book was easy to write* and *Writing the book was easy* – may share a central meaning and yet express contextual distinctions. One of the hidden principles of style is the selection of the form that best fits the context.

There is, in fact, a *repertoire* of items, idioms, constructions and grammatical processes, which every competent user of the language commands. Repertoire choices can in many instances be reduced to simple oppositions, e.g. the 'marked' versus the 'normal' order of elements in a declarative sentence:

Thirty miles they marched that day

versus

They marched thirty miles that day.

Or the active versus the passive:

The decision angered us all

versus

We were all angered by the decision.

Or the declarative versus the existential sentence-form:

The House was in uproar

versus

There was uproar in the House.

Or the extraposition versus its inversion:

It is all too obvious that mice eat cheese

versus

That mice eat cheese is all too obvious.

Or the simple versus the cleft sentence:

The knave stole the tarts

versus

It was the knave who stole the tarts.

Or the participle clause versus the adverbial clause:

> His work finished / Having finished his work, he drank three beers in quick succession

versus

> When he had finished his work, he drank three beers in quick succession.

Or the embedding of the infinitive versus the participle clause:

> To paint in watercolours requires great skill

versus

> Painting in watercolours requires great skill.

But the list might be continued through many pages, only to be rewritten many times over, as the permutations of these simple pairings are explored.

Let us call a halt here, with the clear emergence of an important principle, that of *choice*. Being at liberty to choose is the real problem of usage, the central difficulty of style. We do not say of the alternatives listed above, that one of each pair is wrong or inferior or infelicitous while the other is correct or commendable. If asked in each case to express a preference, we would begin, no doubt, to postulate contexts and purposes. Grammar evolves in response to complex motivations and demands; style expresses the freedom and the discipline of exercising options among the profusion of grammatical forms. In all this there is little room for simple rules and recommendations. The more we consider the elaboration of language, the more naive must prescriptiveness appear. Nevertheless, we cling in hope and doubt to the notion that some principles may be usefully prescribed, as a basis for sound stylistic practice. This is the theme of our next chapter.

# 3
# Prescriptions

Rules and models destroy genius and art.
– William Hazlitt

You write with ease, to show your breeding,
But easy writing's vile hard reading.
– R.B. Sheridan

### 1 A basic style?

Prescriptions are rules of verbal conduct, sometimes supported by argument, sometimes dogmatically laid down: e.g. that we should avoid the passive, not use too many adverbs, steer clear of verbs ending in -*ize*. What is frequently baffling about such pronouncements is their refusal to concede the possibility of turning your style to suit your purpose. We are warned absolutely against this word, encouraged totally on behalf of that construction, until we receive the impression that there is only one style worthy of the name, whether we write a learned treatise or a letter to Uncle Podger. Edicts of 'never' and 'always' override the caution (and truthfulness) of 'it all depends'.

It does all depend, of course. It depends on the convenience of speech, the reflective strictness of writing, the formality of a situation, the progression of a text, the intimacy of participants in discourse (speaker-listener, writer-reader), the assertions of a personality, the desire to inform, to question, to direct, to imply, to persuade, to entertain, even to deceive. There are many determinants of style, and many acts of communication are stylistically complex. It might then seem artificial to propose a distinction between 'first-level' and 'second-level' problems of usage, and to presume, as a working notion, the existence of a basic style. At the outset, however, there is some value in the assumption of primary rules and procedures which the writer may set aside only under special circumstances. What we practise at this 'first level' is a style intended to cope efficiently with ordinary transactions, simple reports, arguments, analyses, announcements, directives. These day-to-day purposes leave much to the individuality of the writer, but still are governed by one or two principles of primary competence.

## 2 Coherence

The first necessity is a coherent text. Every sentence should be firmly constructed, each part standing in clear relationship to the rest, so that the meaning emerges unambiguously and there is no vagueness of wording to puzzle the reader for a single moment. This is an exacting skill, in which all writers must at times falter. When the design is botched through haste, or for want of proper forethought, the text drifts towards incoherence:

> While so many people continuously moan about ever increasing prices – albeit at a lower rate these days – in so many areas, the truth is that in the private sector science and the market place have combined to see a whole host of technological marvels come down in price in recent years – from pocket calculators, digital watches, home computers, to, now, the video.
>
> (*Daily Telegraph*)

Journalists are hard-pressed to produce their copy quickly, and it is perhaps a little unfair to turn to these hasty compositions for examples of mismanaged writing. Nevertheless, this piece of editorial comment from a national newspaper is certainly a flawed construction, a complex sentence that sets out to summarize an argument, but flounders badly.

The first clause is particularly inept:

> While so many people continuously moan about ever-increasing prices – albeit at a lower rate these days – in so many areas . . .

## Prescriptions

The mistaken use of *continuously* for *continually* makes an unintended joke. The real problem, however, is the clumsy parenthesis and the failure to establish unambiguously the pattern of adverbial elements in the clause. Do we suppose the writer to mean that *people continuously moan, albeit at a lower rate these days*, or that *prices are ever-increasing, albeit at a lower rate these days*? The first supposition raises the question of how to measure a rate of moaning, particularly if the moaning is continuous. The second presents the paradox (not unknown to government spokesmen and political apologists) of prices that are ever-increasing at a lower rate, getting higher slower and making us richer as we grow poorer. Neither interpretation makes a great deal of sense. Further, do *people moan in so many areas*, or are *prices increasing in so many areas*? This prompts the further question of what is meant here by that vogue word, *area*: a space (*People are continuously moaning in Sainsbury's car park*), a department of business or public life (*People are continuously moaning in the Civil Service*), or a type of commodity (*People are continuously moaning about the price of a drink*)?

The remainder of the sentence is not quite so badly managed, but still makes heavy going of what should be a relatively easy course. Consider, for example:

> science and the market place have combined to see a whole host of technological marvels come down in price . . .

The writer evidently feels that in metonymy lies power: *science* and *the market place*, not 'scientists' and 'salesmen'. This rhetoric, however, results in an oddly unsatisfactory configuration, suggesting a 'combination' of entities that do not very obviously 'combine'. (One might as well say that *Religion and the hearse have combined to see a whole host of people interred*.) Assuming such a combination to be admissible, however, or reading 'scientists' and 'salesmen' for *science* and *the market place*, there is yet another query: do parties *combine* to *see* (or *watch* or *observe* or *experience*) an event? The following examples are idiomatically dubious (to say the least):

> Education and the stock market combined to observe the rise of the middle class.

> Tom and Bert combined to see their team win.

'Combine to' surely implies a resultant action, process, development, etc.;

> Good teachers and clever businessmen combined to ensure the rise of the middle class.

> Tom and Bert combined to score the winning goal.

These irregularities do not prevent us from grasping the intended meaning, but they are irritating, as minor kinks of language making small semantic knots in the text. There is yet another tangle towards the end of the text, where the bracketing *from . . . to* construction is improperly used. Strictly speaking, this construction should not introduce a list, but only identify extremes or termini. Thus we might say:

> The whole family was there, from old Grandpa Bloggs to little baby Susan

not

> The whole family was there, from old Grandpa Bloggs, Aunt Sarah, Aunt May, Uncle Jim, Cousin Alf, Mum, Dad, Jessie, Jessie's boyfriend Sid, Margaret, Cissie, young Jack, to, most recently, baby Susan.

The *from . . . to* bracket is pointless if a detailed list is supplied. It may even be misleading because of its customary implication of some sort of polarity (*from the richest to the poorest, from the oldest to the youngest, from the tallest to the shortest, from the very primitive to the highly sophisticated, everything from a pin to a piano*, etc.). Possibly the writer of the editorial meant us to infer that pocket calculators were the *first* technological marvel to come down in price, followed by digital watches, then by home computers, and *lastly* by video players, so that *from . . . to* implies 'from earliest to most recent'; but this interpretation is not really justified by the text, which confusedly blends two processes, that of indicating a span and that of presenting an inventory.

The text is not incoherent in the sense of being unintelligible. Cursorily read, it makes a lump of meaning: *Everyone complains that prices keep going up. The truth is that in the private sector some prices are coming down, Thanks to technology and shrewd commerce we are now paying less for pocket calculators, digital watches, home computers, and video machines.* It is only when the text is read with the attention demanded by an editorial in a 'quality' newspaper that this meaning dissolves in the ambiguities and false relationships of the language that purports to express it. In that sense the text is incoherent.

### 3 Simplicity

Coherence is often threatened when a writer tries to make a unit of text carry more than it will conveniently hold. This is one of the commonest breaches of the basic principle of *simplicity*. Here is an example:

> Writers on the philosophical aspects of perception rarely concern themselves with illusions or hallucinations involving any other sense than vision, but if we are to learn about the status of hallucinations in general this is unduly restricting, and may be actually misleading, if there turn out to be certain features peculiar to hallucinations in the sphere of vision which, in the absence of information about other forms of hallucinations, might be taken to be characteristic of hallucinations in general.
> (Sir Russell Brain, *The Nature of Experience*).

This complex sentence creates no ambiguities, and will be seen to be logically constructed, if one has the tenacity to follow its argument through a chain of subordinations-within-subordinations. Therein lies its fault; by the time the construction has proceeded from *but if* to *this*, to *if* again (introducing an existential proposition in the subjunctive mood, *if there turn out to be*), then on to a *which*-clause, travelling through a parenthesis (*in the absence of information*, etc.) before arriving at a passive with a modal auxiliary (*might be taken*), the reader is a little disorientated.

The text can be simplified – which does not mean that it can be made available to simpletons. Its technical abstractions will remain, and its syntax cannot be reduced to the nursery level of drastically simple sentences. Nevertheless, some simplification can be attempted. To begin with, it can be broken into three separate sentences, preserving the original wording:

> (1) Writers on the philosophical aspects of perception rarely concern themselves with illusions or hallucinations involving any other sense than vision.
>
> (2) If we are to learn about the status of hallucinations in general this is unduly restricting.
>
> (3) It may be actually misleading, if there turn out to be certain features peculiar to hallucinations in the sphere of vision which, in the absence of information about other forms of hallucinations, might be taken to be characteristic of hallucinations in general.

This makes the text a little easier to follow, but only a little; it exposes the problem without offering a wholly acceptable solution. Sentence 3 of this breakdown comprises the most awkward part of the original text, and it remains teasingly complex, defying reduction as long as its wording is kept intact. Then the next step must be to revise the wording along with the syntax. Here is a version:

> Writers on the philosophical aspects of perception rarely concern themselves with hallucinations involving any sense other than vision. This is unduly restricting if we are to learn about the status of hallucinations in general. It may even be misleading, if we consequently assume that certain features of visual hallucination are also characteristic of other forms, about which we have no information.

This version simplifies the text with no appreciable reduction of its content. One highly complex sentence has been broken into three somewhat less complex units. There is one important change of branching, i.e. from the left-branch of *if we are to learn . . . this is unduly restricting* to the right-branch of *this is unduly restricting if we are to learn*. This change is made for the sake of firmer textual cohesion (on cohesion, see p.40). There is also some reformulation, or 'translation' – e.g. *turn out to be* is expressed in a different way by *consequently*, and the cautious, modally coloured passive *might be taken to be* is re-phrased by the straightforwardly active *we assume that*.

These simple changes have produced a somewhat clearer text. Its relative simplicity has been brought about (a) by analysing the content, i.e. by asking whether it might be divided into segments or phases, and (b) by looking at the most direct and compact way of presenting this segmentation. As a footnote to the exercise, it must be said that this extract is taken from the printed text of a lecture. What we have here may therefore be an imperfect compromise between the improvisations of spoken address, with its straggle of *if*s, *and*s, *but*s, and *which*es (any lecturer will recognize the symptoms), and the tidier regime of writing. 'Tidiness', indeed, is the object, and were it not for cosy domestic connotations, the word might serve our purposes better than *simplicity*. A complicated text may still be tidy.

### 4 Compactness

Tidy expression is compact expression; and this is achieved partly by cutting out the unnecessary word, partly by finding the brief equivalent of the expanded phrase. Writing of a talkative kind, e.g. the language of sports correspondents, is often rather loosely constructed:

> It looks touch and go, however, whether Hoddle will be fit to tour South America with England in June – and it could also interfere with his prospects of joining a top international club during the summer.
> 
> (*The Times*)

> Having survived by the skin of their teeth at Gosforth in the last round of the John Player Special Cup, Wasps will not be smiling at the prospect of facing a daunting task at Orrell this Saturday minus three of their regular backs.
> 
> (*Guardian*)

These sentences exemplify a peculiar semi-colloquial semi-literary style which is acceptable in the context of the sports page, where it is recognized and even enjoyed as a distinctive genre. Criticism may therefore be disarmed; nevertheless, these examples can be improved. The first might be rewritten thus:

Hoddle's injury, however, could exclude him from England's tour of South America in June, and could also prevent him from joining a major foreign club during the summer.

In the original text there is no obvious antecedent for the second *it* (in *it could also interfere*, etc.; on antecedence, see p.59). In the revised version, *injury* is the unmistakable subject of the two coordinated clauses. Other changes produce a firmer, less 'wordy' reading: *could* obviates *looks touch and go whether*, and *prevent him from* subsumes *interfere with his prospects of*. As for the second example, what prospects beyond prospects are contained in the phrase *smiling at the prospect of facing*, i.e. smiling at the prospect of having something in prospect, or smiling at a prospective prospect? To say that someone will not be smiling at the prospect of facing a daunting task is as absurd as to say that they will be scowling at the idea of considering an unpleasant thought. A revision might read:

> Having barely survived at Gosforth in the last round of the John Player Special Cup, Wasps will not look forward to playing at Orrell this Saturday without three of their regular backs.

For any journalistic fault we can always find the excuse of haste to meet the call for copy. That plea cannot be made on behalf of academic portentousness, of the kind reflected in sentences like these:

> Despite the successful establishment of the scheme as mentioned above, it is clear that there is considerable spare capacity in terms of the video replay network.

> Needless to say, where a gap is seen to have developed between teaching and learning it is logical to attempt to close the gap by diagnosing student weaknesses and by providing students with help and guidance concerning remedial learning.
>
> (*Teaching at a Distance*, no. 23, issed by the Open University)

It is remarkable that so much flaccid English should be

written by educationists; these are by no means rare examples. The first could be rewritten:

> Despite the general provision of video replay machines, they are seldom used

or:

> Although there are plenty of video replay machines, few people use them.

And the second:

> Needless to say, if students are not learning what they are taught, we should find out why, and try to help them.

'Needless to say', indeed; when the message is reduced to simple terms it seems hardly worth transmitting. Such revisions often criticize a thought as much as they criticize the language in which it is couched. The author of the second example might object that *remedial learning* is an appropriate technical term, but it is not readily apparent that *help them* says less than *provide with help and guidance concerning remedial learning*. I ask my doctor to *cure me* or *help me get better*, not to *provide me with help and guidance concerning the recuperative process*.

## 5 Discretion

Acceptable prescriptions will be those that make for coherent, simple, compact writing. There is one other quality to consider. How far should a writer allow a personality, with all its whims, heats, ironies, eccentricities, to be displayed in his text? Here are some examples of writing that advertises the presence of the writer:

> The traditional Springtide wails can be heard from the Greater London Tories as the customary grants to batty left-wing groups are dished out by the Ken and his henchpersons.
> 
> (*Guardian*)

> Marilyn, one pauses respectfully, imagining those football

buttons cascading down that bust, was the other half of The Other Half (BBC 1).

At least, that I imagine is the way it was meant to be as Victor Lowndes is the former boss of the Playboy Club and usually described as a colourful millionaire while Marilyn is only a retired bunny with a nice line in gentlemen-prefer-playmates chat. (*Guardian*)

All the specimens yet mentioned have been productions of individual caprice: the writer for some reason or other took a liberty, or made a mistake, with one expression; he might as well, or as ill, have done it with another, enjoying his little effect, or taking his little nap, at this moment or at that. (H.W. and F.G. Fowler, *The King's English*)

The first passage is from a political 'diary' column, the second from a review of television programmes. Their styled and self-conscious chattiness, like the talkative tenor of the sports commentator, is appropriate to a genre; the object in each case is to amuse the reader for a moment, in reference to ephemeral things. (Perhaps even now *the Ken* must be glossed; it refers to Mr Ken Livingstone, socialist leader of the Greater London Council.) The stylistic display is characterized by a free mingling of 'literary' (e.g. *Springtide*) and extremely colloquial words (e.g. *batty, dished out*); by a heavy jocosity – Mr Livingstone gets the honorific article, *the Ken*, as though he were some Highland chieftain; by a coy intrusion of the authorial self (*one pauses respectfully*); and by some arch and artful word-play (*henchpersons* for *henchmen*, parodying the vocabulary of the Women's Movement; *gentlemen-prefer-playmates* recalling the phrase 'gentlemen prefer blondes' and alluding to the naked girls of *Playboy* magazine, demurely styled 'playmates').

The third passage obviously does not fall into this category of cute words for keen consumers. It is an extract from a classic textbook, chosen from a section in which the authors examine and criticize the neologisms of various writers, among them Thomas Carlyle, George Meredith, and Herbert Spencer. This is a matter of some substance and solemnity. Yet even here there is a hint of personality, particularly in the phrases *enjoying his little effect, or taking his little nap*. *Nap* is a mischievous lapse into the colloquial, and *little* patronizes some distinguished authors. 'They *will* do it, these people who should know better' is the message spoken, *sotto voce*, by this text. A personality emerges (not too agreeably) from the passage, but as an incidental quality of the writing, not as the principal object. We may perhaps distinguish between self-expression and *posturing*. The whole purpose of the first two examples is to strike the entertaining posture.

Vigour and high spirits can be very desirable qualities in writing, and certainly we must not assume that all departures from a flat non-committal style are examples of culpable affectation. Many styles, among them the most distinguished, are 'affected', and in no bad sense; to put on a mask, take on a role, is one of the writer's legitimate functions. We should never wear the mask vainly, however. We must use discretion, tempering the manner to the topic, observing what our older rhetoricians called a *decorum*.

## 6 Prescriptions

A style cannot be made by rule or taught by recipe, but some prescriptions may still be necessary. What follows here is a list of recommendations, to each of which some explanatory comment is added. The first prescription, dealing with matters of elementary care, should be observed at all times; the rest apply under conditions noted in the commentary.

Prescription 1 *The components of a sentence must be clearly and unambiguously related*

In particular, note the following points:

(a) Verbs agree with their subjects, in the category of *number* (i.e. as singular or plural). Thus *a code of principles have been drafted* is incorrect, because the formal subject of the sentence is *code* (requiring *has*), not the plural *principles*. This is an example of 'false agreement' or 'false concord'. In such a simple illustration, the point may seem obvious; nevertheless the error is not uncommon. Writers (and also typists and compositors) are often misled by items in proximity; thus *a code of principles* may prompt the false agreement because the item immediately preceding the verb (i.e. *principles*) is plural. Collective nouns (e.g. *set, series, number, class, committee, government*) offer occasional problems of interpretation:

> A group of solicitors are planning to set up the first solicitors' property centre in England.
> (*Daily Telegraph*)

*Group* is singular and requires a singular form of the verb. However, this sentence could be excused the charge of false agreement if it were argued that *group* here refers to a number of individuals rather than an entity. Words like *class* have this ambivalence: *The class was unruly* is 'correct' if *class* is seen as referring to a unit, while *The class were amused* is equally correct, if *class* is taken to refer to the people comprising the unit. Simple failures of concord, or apparent anomalies, rarely puzzle the reader. The usual response to a lapse of subject–verb concord is one of irritation or scornful amusement at an evident illiteracy. Breaches of subject–complement agreement usually escape censure:

> The measures are regarded as an indication of General Zia's nervousness about opposition to his regime. (*Daily Telegraph*)

It would be a severe critic who, noting the lapse of agreement between *measures* (plur.) and *indication* (sing.), would demand the revision: *The measures are regarded as indicating General Zia's nervousness*, etc.

(b) When the subject of a sentence is elaborately and carelessly realized, there is a danger that the sentence will lose coherence and that the reader will be misled. An example:

> The commitment, sharp competitive edge and not least ability of almost all the juniors and not just the finalists to hit skilful spectacular winners, made it a heartening weekend. (*Daily Telegraph*)

The structure is $SVOC_o$, thus:

S: The commitment, sharp competitive edge and not

least ability of almost all the juniors and not just the
finalists to hit skilful spectacular winners
V: made
O: it
C$_o$: a heartening weekend.

This breakdown shows the elaborate realization of S in a front-weighted sentence (on 'front-weighting' see further pp. 77, 87). The general sense may be outlined as *The commitment, competitive spirit, and skill of all the junior players made it a heartening weekend*. The sense of structure is lost, however, in the elaboration of a triple subject, the headwords of which are *commitment*, *edge*, and *ability*. The elaboration is inelegant and idiomatically questionable. *Not least* seems to require an article or a possessive pronoun before the following noun. (Thus, *The Women's Institute, the church choir, and not least the Brownies contributed to the success of the afternoon*, or *Fluency, skill in composition, and not least an ability to please public sentiment made him a fashionable painter*.) *Not just* comes confusingly in the wake of *not least* and *almost all*. The *and* of *almost all the juniors and not just the finalists* is a further source of confusion, since it might prompt the inference that the juniors and the finalists are separate groups of people; a better reading would be almost *all the juniors, not just the finalists*. The major problem, however, it is the awkward length of a noun phrase with a postmodifying sequence into which a non-finite clause is embedded: *ability of almost all the juniors and not just the finalists to hit skilful spectacular winners*. A little punctuation would ease the burden of this: *the ability of almost all the juniors, not just the finalists, to hit skilful spectacular winners*. This does not entirely smooth the reader's path, and there remains in the sentence a shadow of ambiguity, in that the infinitive clause *to hit skilful spectacular winners* is apparently governed not only by *ability* but also by *commitment* and *competitive edge*. It is possible to rewrite the sentence, keeping the long S, but clearly articulating its three component elements:

The commitment of the players, their sharp competitive edge, and not least the ability to hit skilful spectacular winners, shown not only by the finalists but by almost all the juniors, made it a heartening weekend.

The ponderous front-weighting remains, but the sentence is no longer confusing or ambiguous.

(c) Syntactic concord and semantic concord go together; the grammatical frame links compatible references. The principle calls for illustration. An example, therefore:

> The recognition by Barnes that, no matter residence in Wales since early childhood and schooling at Bassaleg, he was English in thought and deed, was a happy day for English rugby – besides being a heart-felt tribute to his splendid Welsh mentors.
>
> (*Daily Telegraph*)

The gist of the sentence appears to be that Barnes, brought up in Wales, happily decided to be an English rugby player; otherwise it is difficult to make much sense of it. The structure is SVC, with the words *The recognition . . . thought and deed* as S. The element C is realized by *a happy day*, etc., and then, in the appended participle clause, by *a heart-felt tribute*, etc. Thus there are two basic propositions:

> The recognition that he was English was a happy day for English rugby.

> The recognition that he was English was a heart-felt tribute to his splendid Welsh mentors.

The objection to the first of these is that a *recognition* is not *a happy day*. These are semantic incompatibles; one might say with comparable absurdity that *The concept of curved space was an exciting time for physics*. It is of course acceptable to write *It was a happy day for English rugby when Barnes recognized*, etc.; in that case the syntactic form marches with the semantic intention. The second proposition requires us to attribute to *recognition* the meaning of 'something expressed': *In recognizing the fact that he was English* (= 'while putting his recognition into words') *he also paid heartfelt tribute to his Welsh mentors*. This concrete/dynamic sense of the word is at variance with the abstract/stative sense it bears in the first proposition. Two meanings are smudged into one in this sentence.

One other blunder may be mentioned. It occurs within the

parenthetical sequence *no matter residence in Wales since early childhood and schooling at Bassaleg*. The wording falsely suggests a conjunction of *early childhood* and *schooling at Bassaleg*, i.e. *He had lived in Wales ever since his early childhood and his schooling at Bassaleg*. The true conjunction is, of course, that of *residence* and *schooling*: *He had lived in Wales ever since early childhood, and had been schooled at Bassaleg*. One way of removing this ambiguity would be to replace *early childhood* by a premodifier (to *residence*), thus limiting unmistakably the reference of *and*: *despite his lifelong residence in Wales and his schooling at Bassaleg*.

(c) The importance of the small grammatical words must by now be evident; it is essential that their reference and scope should be exclusively clear. It should not be possible to mistake the *antecedent* of a pronoun or preposition, i.e. the part of speech on which it properly depends. When the antecedent is misread, the meaning of the sentence is called into question. Thus, *The officers ordered the men to clean their quarters* is ambiguous, because it is not clear – without information from a supporting context – whether *their* refers to *men* or *officers*. Given the sentence as it stands, a reader might very well assume the nearer word, *men*, to be the more likely reference. This psychological rule of proximity affects more than one grammatical pattern in English. The separation of a preposition from its antecedent is a potent source of ambiguity, much exploited by humorists:

> Among the exhibits was an ingeniously constructed gaming table for up to eight players with detachable legs.

The antecedent of *with* is *table*, not *players*, a fact that the unlucky ordering of the sentence momentarily conceals. Sober sense cannot, however, be wholly restored by putting the phrase *with detachable legs* next to its antecedent, *table*:

> Among the exhibits was an ingeniously constructed table with detachable legs for up to eight players.

New problems of antecedence arise (*detachable legs for up to eight players?*) because table 'governs' *for* as well as *with*. What is needed is some careful punctuation, or, if a well-placed comma is unavailing, a rewording of the entire sentence. Punctuation is not always the answer, as the following remarkable example shows:

> Handsome brickie Tony Barker cemented an amazing bond as he lay dying . . . between his wife and his mistress. (*Sun*)

The dots suggest an uncomfortable awareness of the ambiguity lurking in this treacherous construction. The proposed antecedent of *between* must be *cemented* ('he cemented a bond between them'), not *lay dying* ('he lay dying between his wife and mistress'); yet the hastily defensive punctuation will not prevent the amused reader from taking the sentence in the latter sense. It is easy enough to avoid the ambiguity by slightly re-ordering the construction:

> As he lay dying, handsome brickie Tony Barker cemented an amazing bond . . . between his wife and his mistress.

The dots now serve a different purpose – perhaps the one originally intended; they express the pause that precedes a revelation, explanation, or definition. The sentence is still absurd, because of the silly play on *cement* and *bond*, but at least it is unambiguously absurd.

(d) Be particularly careful in relating a main clause and a dependent participle clause, adjectival clause, verbless clause, or disjunct. Here are some cautionary examples, mostly noted from TV news transmissions:

> (1) On reaching Kenya, our problems were not over. (ITN news broadcast)

(Here is the classic error of the 'dangling participle'; it is not 'our problems' that reach Kenya. The well-worn classroom example is *Coming to school, a bus nearly ran over me.* Re-cast: *Coming to school, I was nearly run over by a bus*; and similarly, *On reaching Kenya, we found that our problems were not over.*)

> (2) Once having gained sufficient interest locally, a harder socialist message can be introduced. (*Guardian*)

(It is not the 'socialist message' that gains local interest. Replace the participle clause with an adverbial clause: *When sufficient local interest has been attracted*, etc.)

(3) Observed from the shore, negotiations for the hijacked vessel continue. (TV news broadcast)

(It was in fact the vessel that was being observed from the shore while the negotiations were taking place. Again, rewrite with an adverbial clause: *Negotiations continue while the hijacked vessel is observed from the shore.*)

(4) Standing behind her, a bearded Armenian shouted instructions, a pistol held close to her head. (TV news broadcast)

(The introductory participle clause is correctly related to its main clause, *a bearded Armenian shouted instructions*. It is at the end that the sentence loses its way. Was the Armenian a bearded lady intent on suicide? Read: *Standing behind her and holding a pistol close to her head, a bearded Armenian shouted instructions.*)

(5) I made records of her talking, unaware that she was being recorded. (Student's essay)

(Who was 'unaware', 'she', or 'I'?)

(6) If successful, this will be the first panda born by artificial insemination outside China. (TV news magazine)

(It is the insemination that needs to be successful, whether outside China or outside the Savoy Hotel. The sentence misrelates *if successful* with *panda*.)

(7) Like London in 1851, there was an atmosphere of pride and optimism. (TV Broadcast)

(*Like London in 1851* is not properly related to the main clause. Two rewritings are possible: *As in London in 1851, there was an atmosphere of pride and optimism* – making clear the adverbial link with the verb *was*; or *There was an atmosphere of pride and optimism, like that of London in 1851*. *Like* presupposes the comparison of *nominal* expressions.)

(8) Like Tweedledum and Tweedledee, different governments have pummelled and undermined our top industries and it is absurd. (Reader's letter in *The Times*)

(But Tweedledum and Tweedledee did not pummel and undermine anyone's top industries; they pummelled each other. In this case, a corrected version is elusive, because the underlying thought is confused. Possibly: *Indistinguishably aggressive as Tweedledum and Tweedledee, different parties in government have made our leading industries the object of their battle*. But it would have been better to forget dum and dee.)

It might be said of any of these instances except, perhaps, the last, that the meaning comes over clearly enough, despite the flaws of grammatical form. True; but it is none the less dangerous to permit any inadequate matching of form and content. Concede the elementary and obvious case, and the subtler error, more disruptive of meaning, may the more readily creep in.

Prescription 2 *Keep a clear syntactic line; try not to lose your reader in constructional mazes*

This prescription has been anticipated to some extent in comments on coherence and the dangers of the elaborated subject. It is rather easy to fall into the habit of making syntactic digressions and interpolations. Here is a cautionary example from a critical review of an art exhibition:

> Its rows of sequential photographs, pictures and sculptures subscribe to the now derided – in this new age of uncertainty – clinical certitude of Structuralism. And of course in the metaphorical waffle of its 'Pier +' spatially infinite 'Ocean' title, in its tendency to set the isolated moment against mind-boggling eternities – best exemplified by one artist who does nothing but send telegrams (subsequently retrieved and framed) from all over the world to his friends saying only 'I am alive' – in its general preoccupation with making static representations of time and interlude, it betrays the influence of the Space programme, then at its zenith. (*Spectator*)

This is, in its own word, mind-boggling. The stem of the second sentence is represented by the words *And of course . . . it betrays the influence of the Space programme*. Between the disjunct *of course* and the main clause *it betrays*, etc., there are three long adverbial constructions (*in the metaphorical waffle*, etc.; *in its tendency to set*, etc.; *in its preoccupation with*, etc.). Two of these are separated by a long parenthesis (*best exemplified by*, etc.), which in its turn is interrupted by another parenthetical expression (*subsequently retrieved and framed*). The management of the sentence, as a sequence of parallel constructions, is seriously impaired by these interruptions. It even appears that the title 'Pier + Ocean' is breached parenthetically by the critic's own explanatory comment, *spatially infinite*. The fragmentation of the syntax, and the unwieldy length of phrase, can only confuse the reader.

Prescription 3 *Avoid loose, comma-connected strings of independent clauses*

Here is a prescription that requires careful illustration. Certain famous passages of English prose exploit with sonorous effect 'comma-connected strings of independent clauses':

> We shall fight in France, we shall fight on the seas and the oceans, we shall fight with growing confidence and growing strength in the air, we shall defend our island, whatever the cost may be, we shall fight on the beaches, we shall fight on the landing grounds, we shall fight in the fields and in the streets, we shall fight in the hills. (Sir Winston Churchill)

But this is a planned rhetorical scheme, and no one could suppose that its progression of parallel constructions is anything other than deliberate. Quite different is the merely casual hitching together of clauses into a slack sequence:

> The prescription directs you not to write like this, only slovens and people with no aesthetic sense write like this, it makes dismal reading, the merest child can see how bad it is.

Writers of fiction may construct such sentences *mimetically*, in echoing a style of speech or in representing the flow of a character's thoughts. In non-fictional prose this bemused rambling is a vice.

Prescription 4 *Avoid the mannerism of the 'snapped' sentence – the headless predicate, the tailless subject, the brute interjection*

There may sometimes be stylistic justification for writing a verbless clause, or one from which the subject has been deleted, or one in which an adverbial or a complement stands for the whole sentence-process. This can be an effective representation of the powerful, incisive comment. It is, however, a potent, not to say strident, device, and a very little of it goes a long way:

> That clipped style. Terse. Giving the impression of laconic strength. Not wasting words. Getting through to him. The reader. Keeping him on his toes. Driving him. Right out of his mind, probably.

Some tricks of style are like spices; you must know when to use them, and you need only a pinch. This is one such. Note the device, therefore, but do not let an occasional turn become a tedious habit.

Prescription 5 *In your concern for coherence and simplicity, do not overwork the conjunctions 'and', 'but', 'for', 'so', 'then', 'yet', 'because', 'as'*

There is a traditional distinction between 'loose' and 'periodic' sentence structure. The 'loose' structure is perfectly respectable as a stylistic resort; the designedly 'loose', however, is not to be confused with the shiftlessly 'lax':

> Of course we should visit the dentist regularly, but we should also be responsible for our own oral hygiene, and that means daily brushing, so brush your teeth at least once a day; yet do not neglect the gums, because they must also be kept healthy, as it is round the rims of the teeth and the gums that plaque forms. Then the enamel is attacked, so your teeth decay, and you have to go to the dentist again.

The naive conjunctive rattle of *and . . . then . . . so . . . because* is often a feeble attempt to avoid the comma-connecting illustrated under Prescription 3. A very different matter is the planned simplicity of *and, then, so, because*, etc., in skilled narrative:

> The old man made the sheet fast and jammed the tiller. Then he took up the oar with the knife lashed to it. He lifted it as lightly as he could because his hands rebelled at the pain. Then he opened and closed them on it lightly to loosen them. He closed them firmly so they would take the

pain now and would not flinch and watched the sharks come. (Ernest Hemingway, *The Old Man and the Sea*)

This, for all its plainness, is elaborately calculated; the prescription has no force in such cases.

Prescription 6 *Avoid stylistic blends; keep unity of tone in vocabulary, do not mix metaphors, respect idiomatic logic*

A simple case of failure to 'keep unity of tone' in vocabulary would be made by the assertion *It's a wise offspring that kens its own poppa*, or *It's an insightful infant that has the low-down on its progenitor*. These absurd examples may at least strike a reader as having humour, of a sort; and indeed, a shift in the level of vocabulary, from the strictly bookish to the freely colloquial, or vice versa, can be a means of creating boldly witty effects. But this must be a 'second level' option. At the first level we try to keep a clear distinction between literary idiom and knockabout talk. They are inelegantly mixed in the following example:

> In a linguistic appropriation that would cause a jolt to the Socialist Workers' Party organisers of the Right to Work marches in Britain, the US 'Right to Work' campaign is a fiercely anti-labour outfit that tries to get individual states to pass 'Right to Work' laws which makes union recognition more difficult. (*New Statesman*)

The primary failure of this sentence is syntactic; it violates at more than one point the requirements of our Prescription 1. If this is 'wrong':

> In a nomenclature that often puzzles foreigners, the British public schools are strictly fee-paying institutions

or this:

> In a terminological transfer that might give the Kremlin a surprise, the Salvation Army is a stubbornly peaceful organization

then this is also wrong:

> In a linguistic appropriation that would cause a jolt to the Socialist Workers' Party organisers of the Right to Work

Marches in Britain, the US 'Right to Work' campaign is a fiercely anti-labour outfit.

'Wrong', that is to say, because the introductory adverbial expression is no more than loosely or impressionistically related to the main clause.

There is also an apparent breach of concord at the end of the sentence: *'Right to Work' laws which makes union recognition more difficult.* This is possibly a misprint – *makes* for *make* – or conceivably the result of omitting a comma that would relate *which*, etc., to *pass*: *tries to get individual states to pass 'Right to Work' laws, which makes union recognition more difficult.*

Apart from these lapses, the text is marred by the writer's failure to control the vocabulary, which lurches indecorously between the almost stilted formality of *linguistic appropriation* and the loose slanginess of *anti-labour outfit*. Words are used confidently, as though each one were vigorously and unmistakably stamped with a clear meaning, yet nothing is quite certain. What is a *linguistic appropriation*? Is it simply the borrowing of a word or phrase? Is illicit borrowing (i.e. *misappropriation*) in some way involved? Are we to understand that the borrowed phrase, having been appropriated or misappropriated, has been misapplied? And what manner of institution, organization, party, faction, group, unit, is an *outfit*? Can a campaign be an outfit? These are not merely whimsical questions; they point to the slapdash that mars the sentence from beginning to end.

The mixed metaphor is a commonplace of overstrained rhetoric. An examination candidate tells of a poet *weaving his pawns into the tapestry of his attack*; a newspaper leader-writer speaks of the *berserk fruits* of the government's economic policy; a reporter writes of a squabble in the art world:

> An unseemly atmosphere flavoured by colourful insults and unsavoury accusations by distinguished figures in the art world has brought to boiling point an antipathy that has been building up for years between Dali's present advisers and friends and those once close to him. (*Daily Telegraph*)

Do not let your antipathy build up, lest a colourfully flavoured atmosphere should bring it to boiling point. Such examples require no further comment. As to what is meant by 'idiomatic logic', here is a curious passage from a student's essay:

> Literary writers rely on an impressionistic grammar of conversation which – for all but intensive caricature – dispenses with the largely incommunicative dross generated by a process of 'thinking on the run', whilst retaining the recognizable syntactic hardcore of this medium.

The sustaining figure, presumably, is intended to be a metallurgical image, contrasting the 'core' of pure metal with the 'dross' formed in smelting (the figurative 'core' being the essential content of conversation, while the 'dross' is the token formula, the hesitant noise, the empty phrase). The student has muddled the image, however, by referring to *hardcore*. This is the layer of coarse, packed rubble used in making the foundation of a road or a building. In the essay, *hardcore* is presented as the literal and figurative counter-term to *dross*; and thus the central metaphor is blurred, or disjointed. The reader is not helped by persistent mismatchings in the vocabulary. An *impressionistic grammar of conversation* is said to *dispense* with *dross*, which is *incommunicative* and which is also *generated* (by *thinking on the run*). It is easy to accept that an impressionistic grammar might 'dispense' with elements having no communicative function; or that a smelting process might 'generate' dross; but not that grammar 'dispenses with' dross, or that dross is 'incommunicative', or that it is generated by 'thinking on the run'. Such collocations are breaches of the idiomatic logic that requires each expression to have its fitting partner.

**Prescription 7** *In formal writing, as well as in formal speech, make it a general principle to avoid stumpwords, jargon, and slang*

Stumpwords are the abbreviations of informal chat (*chat* itself being the stump of *chatter*):

> The prof broke his specs at the Lit. Soc. do.

> Twin carbs boost the revs and get you past those artic lorries.

> The house is absolutely fab – all mod cons, a fridge, a telly, and a lime-green lav.

Stumpwords enter a lottery for acceptance into literary and formal usage; *mob* (*mobile vulgus*) has survived into standard from the eighteenth century, while *bam* (*bamboozle*), from the same period, has not. So *fridge* may become a standard item and *fab* may fade (indeed has already faded) with the years. It is not the writer's business to act as arbiter or promoter, however, other than by conservatively avoiding the use of stumpwords in formal English.

Jargon invites the same caution. We know that one person's jargon is another's technical term, and that every occupation has its special vocabulary, items of which sometimes find their way into broader usage. This is part of the ordinary growth of language, and it would be idle to resist the process that gives us, for example, the word *feedback* as a synonym of 'response', 'reaction', 'report'. What should be resisted is the pretentious attribution of scientific weight to quite ordinary statements: *The feedback from our pilot scheme was minimal* = 'We learned little from our first attempt.' In this way *formula* may be jargon, *context* may be jargon, *initiative*, *dialogue* and *parameter* may be jargon:

> In the context of a no-growth situation, the parameters of a meaningful dialogue may be hard to establish, but hopefully the minister's initiative will open the way to a formula for industrial peace.

It is the element of pretentious hectoring that makes such jargon objectionable. Slang may also be a discourtesy to the reader, a mode of jocular bullying that forces his assent:

> A fairly manky-looking cross-section of quacks, shrinks and sawbones had been assembled to discuss euthanasia. (*Spectator*)

For *quacks* read *physicians*, for *shrinks* read *psychiatrists*, for *sawbones* read *surgeons*, for *manky-looking* read *repugnant*; collectively, make the translation *some unattractive representatives of the medical profession*. This short passage (from a review of television programmes) illustrates, indeed, the power and the danger of slang. Its power is to play on feeling, appeal to common-man sympathies, evoke temperamental responses, implant judgments, while it beguiles us with its impudence and colour; its danger lies in its distortions, its exaggerations, its dissatisfaction with discreetly restrained expression.

**Prescription 8** *Make your own phrases; try to avoid cliches and common cant*

In time all expression hardens (or crumbles) into cliché, and it is difficult to write more than a few sentences without having recourse to some well-worn phrase. The danger is not so much that you occasionally let your thought employ a cliché, as that you habitually allow clichés to represent your thought. Swift made joyful war on clichés in his *Polite Conversations*, and another sweetly sardonic Irishman, Myles na Gopaleen (alias Flann O'Brien, alias Brian O'Nolan) composed a superb 'Catechism of Cliché':

> For what occasions does one have a boring and displeasing topic of conversation?
>
> – For breakfast dinner and tea.
>
> From what Aryan prototype do I not know you, sir?
>
> – Adam.
>
> What is the nature of the objection which you have?
>
> – It is rooted
>
> On what is it usual to have one's hours of waiting?
>
> – End.
>
> In what opulent manner does one deserve a thrashing?
>
> – Richly.
>
> With whom is one prepared to take one's chance?
>
> – The next man.

And so on, for many a fecund page. A modern British thesaurus would abound in lustreless phrases from the tarnished word-hoards of journalists, politicians, trade union officials and public relations men. At best harmlessly dull, such expressions can at times have the dangerous power of language-vouchers that rescue the user from the necessity of expending real thought. Therefore never allow your economy to be *blown off course*; eschew the *U-turn*, spare the *swingeing cut*: take no thought for *take-home pay*, shun *the weekly shopping basket*, never hanker after *a package of proposals*, making *substantial offers, in terms of real money, right across the board, at this moment in time*; let nothing appear *at the end of the day*, or even while *it is early days*, and do not permit yourself to see *light at the end of the tunnel* or to *turn the corner*, though of course you should abandon *doom and gloom* (or vice versa) and forget that notorious *winter of discontent*. Grapple with language on your own account, for the sheer pleasure of conquest and possession. (At times you may even *go a bit over the top*.)

Prescription 9 *Try not to be verbose; as a first principle, choose the familiar and concise before the learned and expansive*

What we mean by 'learned' is perhaps open to dispute; Jack's learned word may be Jill's commonplace. It often appears, however, that 'book words' do strange things to the unbookish. A famous rugby player, commenting on the performance of the Welsh side in an international match, says *loose possession is a department they must elaborate in*, meaning *they must try harder to get hold of the ball*. What is the fascination of *elaborate*, that it must be so elaborately sought? And why does *possession* have to be defined as a *department*? Ordinary observations do not gain in value by being dressed in ambitious words.

Put no great trust in polysyllables. Here is a text with a familiar message:

> In summation, let us posit that we have established the invariable relevance (a) of an unconditional confidence in the divine supervision of the human predicament, (b) a firm if rationally unmotivated expectation of a positive issue from situations of a critical nature, and (c) a supportive attitude of committed concern for our various associates – the latter being indisputably the item of paramount importance among these desiderata.

Discerning readers may prefer the simple language of the Authorized Version:

And now abideth Faith, Hope, Charity, these three; but the greatest of these is Charity.

## 7 Purposes

Nine questions of usage have been treated prescriptively. Five of the prescriptions concern syntax, four take up some matters of vocabulary; and that is virtually all that will be said, in this book, about rules of practice. Though the prescriptions are few, they are not, however, randomly made. They serve a purpose which might be described as courtesy in communication.

The syntactic prescriptions require a writer to avoid incoherent, confusing, loose, broken, or misrelated constructions; he is to make his text easy for a reader to follow, clearly demonstrating its connections and its logic. The prescriptions of vocabulary ask the user to be wary of the vogue word, the automatic phrase, the slick, the pretentious, the pert and self-preening, the familiar smirks, winks and nudges that might repel a stranger. The ultimate purport of all these prescriptions is *social*: in public or formal encounters, you must show consideration for those you address. Since what has been said in this chapter applies mainly to writing, the governing principle may be stated as 'Put your reader first'. Putting the reader first demands the cultivation of a coherent, simple, compact style – our 'first level' or 'basic' style.

The reader, however, is not the sole claimant to all the rights of discourse. A second principle might be formulated as 'Serve your subject conscientiously,' and a third as 'Give your personality its due.' Thoughts cannot always be simply expressed, and often the task of presenting a theme with urgency, with conviction, with real power of persuasion, demands that the writer should abandon his discreet and neutral stance. Complex topics and the demand for self-expression imply a 'second level' of style, not definable by *prescription*, but contained in *options*. The distinction between 'first level' and 'second level' is an artifice, of course; one 'level' is involved in the other, and there is no clear line (social or linguistic) to be drawn between them. It is reasonable to claim, however, that some criteria of usage presuppose an *interaction* with a reader (or listener, or 'receiver') while others are related to the *design* of a message, and are thus based on the supposition that there are alternatives to choose from. To these possibilities of choice we now turn.

# 4
# Options

A tale should be judicious, clear, succinct;
The language plain, and incidents well link'd. . .
– William Cowper

. . the shortest way is commonly the foulest, and surely the fairer way is not much about.
– Francis Bacon

**1 Three types**

Beyond the elements of style, choices proliferate. We have the freedom of our language, which includes the freedom to explore the validity of first principles. We may choose, in defiance of prescription, to construct syntactic labyrinths, to string out loose conjunctive lines, to make deliberate shows of jargon and cliché, to mix amazing metaphors. Nevertheless, we must know what we are doing. We must recognize the possibilities and the implications of our choices, so that we do not choose wrongheadedly. Though stylistic options are generally taken by instinct, nimble or stumbling, there are broad possibilities that can be defined and consciously borne in mind; the grounds of instinct, its field of operations, can be objectively drawn. These broad options are listed here under three types, identified as *Distributive Options*, *Presentative Options*, and *Options of Address*. They outline choices recurrently made when style is no longer a 'first level' matter of simple and serviceable documentations, but has shifted to a 'second level' of exhortation, persuasion, polemic, cool rationality, lyrical intensity, narrative guile: to some level of personal art that transcends yet still rests upon the common sense of common usage.

## 2 Distributive options

Our writings carry messages more or less spontaneously loaded into the containers called 'clause' and 'sentence'; we make up, in effect, a syntactic train with vehicles of variable size. Alternatives in packaging are open to us. On the one hand, a great deal may be crammed into a single box; on the other, the same material may be contained in a series of units. The distributive options include the following major possibilities:

Option 1 *The compound sentence-unit versus the sequence of short sentences*

Example:

(1) He brought his relief column to the bank of the river, where the little detachment was still holding out, although its ranks were pitifully depleted, not by enemy action alone, but also by the ravages of disease.

(2) He brought his relief column to the banks of the river. There the little detachment was still holding out. Its ranks, however, were pitifully depleted. This was not the result of enemy action alone. Disease, too, had taken its toll.

Comment:

Example 1 carries its narrative in the large vehicle of one complex sentence, whereas 2 proceeds in a train of simple sentences. Version 2 is perhaps easier to follow at first reading, and therefore is marginally the better response to a 'first level' demand for simplicity. The simplicity is a little forced, however, and the text plods along rather doggedly. For the sake of rhythmical variation it is often advisable to conflate sentences – e.g. *Its ranks were pitifully depleted, not by enemy action alone*. A notable feature of version 2 is that each sentence contains some small item that links it with its predecessor: *there, however, this, too* The role of these words correspond to that of the conjunctions and adverbs (*where, although, not alone . . . but also*) in version 1, i.e. they demonstrate the relations and connections of the text. Some such demonstration is necessary, whether the writer chooses the complex sentence or the sequence of simple units.

## Options

In general, opt for simple sentences –

(a) If each item in a programme of information is to be given equal weight with the others, there being no special prominences or suppressions of prominence.
(b) If the reader is to hold in clear definition the stages of some process, the phases of some development, the terms of some argument.
(c) If the dynamics of expression – whether in reading aloud or in the imaginative reconstruction of silent reading – are designedly 'staccato', with recurrent pauses.
(d) If it is intended to project a distinctive manner or tone of voice, such as laconic matter-of-factness, or dramatic intensity.

Choose the complex unit –

(a) If for the sake of aesthetic proportion and perspective some parts of the message can be brought into prominence while others are conveniently put into a position of reduced emphasis. Compare the relative muting of *not by enemy action alone* in version 1 with the much starker emphasis of *This was not the result of enemy action alone*. The patterning of theme and focus (see 2.7) is affected.
(b) If certain points must be mentioned in passing; less honestly, if there are questions to be adroitly begged. The incidental point or the casual assumption can be framed in a subordinate construction. Note how certain propositions are palmed onto the reader in a sentence such as the following: *The latest proposals, one-sided though they may seem, are designed to control inflation and benefit the whole community by restoring financial confidence, at the acceptable cost of a small rise in the number of those who are for the moment unemployed*. The reader is asked to accept that the interests of one section of the community are those of the whole, that financial confidence is of paramount importance, that a certain level of unemployment is acceptable, and that unemployment is in any case a temporary condition. Acceptance is eased

by a somewhat shifty handling of the argument, shown up by an alternative version in which sentences make stark assertions: *The latest proposals may look one-sided. Nevertheless, they will control inflation and benefit the whole community. They will do that by restoring financial confidence. The cost will be a rise in the numbers of unemployed. The cost is acceptable.*

(c) If the piece is intended in reading, to convey a smooth, fluent, easily paced effect.

The rhythm and dramatic impact of a passage consisting mainly of simple sentences may be enhanced by the introduction of one short, simple unit:

In the past the English used to be accused of complacency, discourtesy, and downright incompetence in their apparent neglect of major European tongues. Their linguistic ability, it seemed, was confined to schoolboy Latin and knowing how to order double whiskies in far-flung colonial outposts. Things have changed. The days of Empire are done, the classics are dying out of the curriculum, and the Englishman, shedding his incompetence with his complacency, is applying himself keenly to the study of French and German.

The short sentence *Things have changed*, unremarkable – indeed banal – as a statement, is powerful as a rhythmic gesture. A much weaker option would have been to incorporate it in a longer sentence, beginning *Things have changed, however, now that the days of Empire are done . . .*

Option 2 *Embedding versus expansion*

Here is a related option. Embedding, discussed in 2.15, packs one pattern inside another; but we can unpack the sentence and redistribute its information in a series of syntactic containers: e.g. we can rewrite *The sound I heard was a scream* as *I heard a sound; it was a scream*. Such 'disembeddings' are here called *expansions*.
Example:

(1) The suggestion from the floor at its annual conference that the Confederation of British Industry get together with the TUC to work out new initiatives in retraining

and employment is imaginative and should not be let slip by the CBI leadership. (*The Times*)

This represents the style of editorial discourse in one of the 'better' newspapers, where such elaborations are not at all uncommon. Embedding is a mark of genteel journalism. The first clause consists of an extended subject (*The suggestion from the floor at its annual conference that the Confederation of British Industry get together with the TUC to work out new initiatives in retraining and employment*), a verb (*is*) and a complement (*imaginative*). This creates a heavily front-weighted construction that might be redistributed and expanded, for example as follows:

(2) At the annual conference of the Confederation of British Industry, the proposal was made from the floor that the CBI and the TUC together should work out new initiatives in retraining and employment. The suggestion is imaginative and should not be let slip by the CBI leadership.

In this version there is an expansion over two sentences. The material from the subject of the first clause in the original text now makes up one sentence-unit. The second sentence in this rewriting corresponds to the coordinated second clause of the original, but a subject (*suggestion*) has been supplied to make a link with the foregoing subject (*proposal*). The pattern is still quite complex, and the process of expansion might be continued, e.g.:

(3) An imaginative proposal was made from the floor at the annual conference of the Confederation of British Industry. This was that the CBI and the TUC together should work out initiatives in retraining and employment. The CBI leadership should not let the suggestion slip.

It may be noticed that in the course of expansion the framing and focusing of the message has changed, very slightly yet enough to modify a reader's impression of what is said. The general recommendation must be, when in doubt (e.g. if the text is at all obscure or cumbersome) expand. There is nevertheless a risk that if the writing is over-expanded the style may lose its tension and compactness, and that the intended emphases may be shifted. These are matters that must be assessed in the larger context of composition.

### Option 3 *Left-branching versus right-branching*

Branching has been discussed, with examples, in 2.14. Options in branching may reflect views of narrative or expository logic, i.e. of the proper sequencing of information, of presuppositions, of cause and effect:

(1) Struggling to my feet and grabbing the fire-extinguisher, I shot a small blob of foam into the fish-pan.

(2) The stove exploded, ripping out the side of the cabin.

The left-branch of 1 is the logical arrangement. A right-branching version – *I shot a small blob of foam into the fish-pan, struggling to my feet and grabbing the fire-extinguisher* – would comically defy the requirements of narrative sequence. The right-branch of 2 is necessary on the same grounds: to say *ripping out the side of the cabin, the stove exploded* would be to put the effective cart before the causal horse. Our presupposition is that destructions follow explosions, not vice versa.

In many cases, therefore, this is a logically determined option. But it can also be a psychological choice, as these examples may suggest:

(Left-branching)
When the skies redden and the sea boils, when fishes climb into the trees, when politicians admit their errors and football hooligans kiss, we will know that the millennium is at hand.

(Right-branching)
Our students are remarkably gifted, even if they read less widely than their predecessors, are less inclined to the play of ideas, more utilitarian in the planning of their studies, more confident in the gospel of efficiency.

Comment:

Left-branching keeps the reader in suspense, often enjoyably, sometimes, perhaps, tediously. He is obliged to wait for, and is challenged to predict, the completion of a message. The distribution has two related disadvantages. One is that it tends to impose on the reader a psychological burden; he must keep mental tally of the subordinate items as he follows the branch towards the stem. The other is that the branch, consequently, cannot be extended at will. There must come a point at which its length begins to confuse and distract. It is no doubt for this reason that elaborate left-branches are often carefully organized in parallel constructions (e.g. the *when . . . when . . . when . . .* of our example). The regular design facilitates the reading.

Right-branching may be protracted to a length that would be intolerable in a left-branch:

> Our students are remarkably gifted, even if they read less widely than their predecessors, are less inclined to the play of ideas, more utilitarian in the planning of their studies, more confident in the gospel of efficiency, and generally disposed to pursue courses of a strictly vocational nature that leave little room for the joys and revelations of speculative enquiry.

Branching of this length is possible because (perhaps only because) language can be recorded in writing; it presents a structure to be kept before the eye and thus the more easily to be held in the mind. The advantage of beginning with the principal item of information (in this case, *our students are remarkably gifted*) is that the psychological tension is eased; the main part of the message is out of the way, and the succeeding subordinated items do not have to be cumulatively recollected. There are dangers (or possibly sly advantages) in this. When the reader is not obliged to bear the whole message cumulatively in mind, he may tend mentally to shed each item as it passes, with the possible result that he loses touch with the basic proposition. An unscrupulous writer might exploit this in order to unbalance an argument or even shift the whole ground of exposition:

> It is of course unthinkable that the death penalty should be reintroduced, notwithstanding the brutality of our society, the daily acts of callous violence, the merciless assaults on

> the old and the weak, the appalling attacks on young children, the cases of rape that have become horrifyingly commonplace, the wickedness that, careless of suffering, rejoices in barbarous deeds of self-indulgence, knowing that it will almost certainly go unpunished.

The end of this sentence is saying something different from the beginning, and by the time the end of the branch is reached, the stem-proposition is almost indiscernibly remote.

Like left-branches, the right-branching text is often brought under the control of some scheme of repetitions or parallels:

> This was a rally of mainly young men, who had been on the picket lines most of the week, who feel a sense of bitter injustice, who want a social revolution, who really believe that this is a police State, and who, having been on strike for five weeks, are also broke. (*Guardian*)

Note that in this case the right-branch, listing the attributes of the 'young men', is virtually obligatory. A left-branching version would be not so much a preference as an awkward contrivance:

> Broke after being on strike for five weeks, really believing that this is a police state, wanting a social revolution, feeling a sense of bitter injustice, standing on the picket lines most of the week, they were mainly young men who attended this rally.

The long introduction comes to a lame conclusion.

Choose the left-branch whenever it seems desirable to postpone or suspend statement of the conclusive element in your message. This is a staple of oratory, and will therefore recommend itself if you are writing a text for performance – e.g. a lecture, a sermon, a speech. Note that this device is often used emotively rather than in demonstrations of plain reasoning; it induces a feeling – a sense of being enjoyably teased, a state of pleasurable expectation, an anticipatory relish.

Use the right-branch when your aim is to state and develop a proposition, particularly if the development is to be at all elaborate. Do not let the branch grow to such a length that when you re-scan your own sentence you find yourself losing the sense of your stem-statement. When in doubt, stop the branch and start a new sentence, using your redistributed material to make a transition. Quite often in the pattern of exposition, sentences branch alternately:

> Britain is still a pleasant place to live in, despite an ailing economy that breeds social unrest. Even though the political parties are divided within themselves, and extremist groups make a periodically violent showing, ours is on the whole a free, democratic, peaceful state.

The main clauses are (a) *Britain is still a pleasant place to live in*, and (b) *ours is on the whole a free, democratic, peaceful state*. These are the stems of successive sentences, between which the branches run, the first sentence being right-branching, the second left-branching.

Option 4 *Mid-branch versus end-branch*

The progress of a sentence may be interrupted by some word, phrase, clause, etc., making a qualification, supplying additional facts, correcting an omission; alternatively, this commentary material may be presented at the beginning or end of the sentence. Examples:

(1) Shelley, for all his love of the sea, never learned to swim

(2) For all his love of the sea, Shelley never learned to swim.

(3) Shelley never learned to swim, for all his love of the sea.

Comment:

Version 1 exemplifies an 'interruptive' pattern: the expression *for all his love of the sea* invades the principal clause *Shelley never learned to swim*. In the other versions this qualification is presented as a left- or right-branch. Those patterns, therefore are not 'interruptive', but 'completive'. (Note that these are not standard grammatical terms, but convenient inventions.) The left-branch of 2 we may call 'pre-completive', the right-branch of 3 'post-completive'. In writing, it is often useful to have the choice of interruptive or completive, although particular cases may impose restrictions on the range of the completive option:

> Some famous novels – *Sons and Lovers* is an example that comes readily to mind – are autobiographical.

In this instance, one independent clause is interrupted by another. It is easy enough to redistribute the clauses in a post-completive pattern. A little punctuation does the trick:

> Some famous novels are autobiographical; *Sons and Lovers* is an example that comes readily to mind.

It is also a simple matter to construct a right-branch with a subordinate clause:

> Some famous novels are autobiographical, *Sons and Lovers* being an example that comes readily to mind.

What seems to be excluded is the pre-completive pattern; e.g. it is hardly acceptable to write: Sons and Lovers *being an example that comes readily to mind, many novels are autobiographical*. A left-branch in this case would require a somewhat different wording and form of the subordinate clause, e.g. *As the example of* Sons and Lovers *readily reminds us, many famous novels are autobiographical*. The sentence might also be recast in the form, Sons and Lovers *comes readily to mind as a famous example of an autobiographical novel*, but in that case the originally subordinate, branching element has become the main clause and the stem of the sentence.

Items that may occur interruptively range from adverbial conjuncts and disjuncts (*however, nevertheless, in fact*, etc.) through qualifying or amplifying phrases and clauses (*for all his love of the sea*; Sons and Lovers *comes readily to mind*), to mid-branches that run through elaborate syntactic sequences:

> Though the centuries of our literature have provided many virtuous rivals, it is still Falstaff, the liar, the impostor, the drunkard, the associate of whores and cutpurses shamelessly presuming on his acquaintance with a prince of the blood royal, the swindler, the graceless white-haired

buffoon, who stands foremost in the ranks of heroically comic characters.

In the second clause of this sentence (*it is still Falstaff . . . who stands foremost in the ranks of heroically comic characters*) there is a long mid-branching sequence of noun phrases, running in one instance to the complexity of a construction with an embedded participle clause (*the associate of whores and cutpurses shamelessly presuming upon his acquaintance with a prince of the blood royal*). Here the mid-branch is undoubtedly the appropriate option. A redistribution would weaken the power of the long qualifying sequence: *It is still Falstaff who stands foremost in the ranks of heroically comic characters, despite the fact that he is a liar, an impostor, a drunkard, the associate of whores and cutpurses shamelessly presuming on his acquaintance with a prince of the blood royal, a swindler, a coward and a graceless white-haired buffoon.* The right-branch turns rhetoric into mere recitation.

A parenthesis, though it may suggest a haphazard drift of discourse, should never occur undesignedly. On the contrary, interruptive constructions should be the most deliberate of stylistic measures. Use them –

(a) Artfully, to suggest the casual afterthought, the hasty concession, the matter to be incidentally mentioned.
(b) Accentually, to isolate the subject or other leading element in a sentence, or to direct emphasis to a minor grammatical item: *Edward Lear – a most moving example – suffered from epilepsy*; *These are not, it should be noted, standard grammatical terms*; *America is still, whatever blemishes her critics may find, a great country.*
(c) 'Suspensively', to postpone momentarily the completion of the sentence, and thus to draw attention to the end-position: *Finally something happened that might be called – with all due respect for the proprieties of language – sensational.*
(d) Rhythmically and echoically, to suggest the pulse and cadence of speech.

## 3 Presentative options

In varying the distribution of material, we often make changes of prominence, drawing the reader's attention to this element or that. A given distribution implies particular characteristics of 'presentation'; the staging of the sentence changes, and with it our view of its properties and its plot. Indeed, as we have seen elsewhere, some striking and stylistically useful changes of presentation can be achieved within the framework of the simple sentence.

**Option 5** *'Normal' ('unmarked') order versus 'Fronted' ('marked') order*

This has been explored in 2.6ff. In writing, the option can be exploited for dramatic alternations of emphasis.
Examples:

(1) The bishop preached a sermon. (SVO normal order)
A very good sermon it was. ($C_s$VS fronted Complement)

(2) Her cooking was excellent. (SV$C_s$ normal order)
Such delicious cakes she baked. (OSV fronted Object)

(3) She grew angry at times. (SV$C_s$A normal order)
On occasion she could be violent (ASV$C_s$ fronted Adverbial)

(4) They made him their leader. (SVO$C_o$ normal order)
President they called him. ($C_o$SVO fronted Object Complement)

(5) I owe Mary my thanks. (SVO$_i$O$_d$ normal order)
Bert I owe nothing. (O$_i$SVO fronted Indirect Object)

Comment:

Such arrangements and rearrangements concern (a) what comes at the beginning of a clause, and (b) what, as a consequence, comes at the end. Each of these positions has a presentative value; the initial position as a place where a topic stands highlighted, the end-position as a denouement, in which the informative 'plot' of the sentence is completed. (Thus, *Our eccentric vicar* may *deliver . . . an abusive sermon; a sharp challenge; a knockout punch; the milk* . . . but only the completion of the clause will show us what.) The end-position is often important as an antecedent base for connection with the next clause or sentence. Compare the following versions:

(1) On the second Sunday after Trinity, before a full congregation, he preached his last sermon. It was on the text 'Blessed are they that mourn.'

(2) His last sermon he preached on the second Sunday after Trinity, before a full congregation. It was on the text 'Blessed are they that mourn.'

The fronted object in 2 raises the dramatic style of the text, but very slightly weakens the linkage of the two sentences. In 1, where *his last sermon* is immediately antecedent to *It* at the beginning of the next sentence, the progression is clearer. Alternations of normal and marked order may sometimes be used to secure the cohesion of a sequence of sentences, linking one to the other heel-and-toe:

Many observers find the economic policy of the government strangely harsh. Harsh it must inevitably be. It would be extraordinarily strange, however, if at this point in her term of office the Prime Minister were to yield to demands for the abandonment of monetary restraint. Concessions and revisions she may allow, but not of the kind that would bring the whole of Conservative policy into disrepute.

In this passage there are four sentences, of which the second and fourth present clauses with fronting (*Harsh it must inevitably, be, Concessions and revisions she may allow*), thus promoting a scheme of phrasal links between sentences:

Sentence 1: Many observers . . . . . . . . . . . . . . . . . . . strangely harsh

Sentence 2: Harsh . . . . . . . . . . . . . . . . . . . . . . . . . . must inevitably be

Sentence 3: would be extraordinarily . . . . abandonment etc.

Sentence 4: Concessions and revisions . . . . . . . into disrepute.

Such links, it will be noted, may consist of a repeated word (*harsh*), an echoed construction (*must be* . . . *would be*), or the contingency of related notions (*abandonment . . . concessions*).

Option 6 *Active versus passive*

One way of shifting the presentative emphasis of a sentence is to change from active to passive voice.

Examples:

(1) Francis scored three goals out of his side's four. (Active)

(2) Three goals out of his side's four were scored by Francis. (Passive)

Comment:

These examples differ in clause structure (SVO, SVA), and in the items realizing the subject (in the one case the subject is *Francis*, in the other *Three goals*). In these formal differences there is an important difference of narrative emphasis. Each sentence, it may be said, presents a theme followed by a story. (Or a topic followed by a comment: compare *Good old Francis! He scored three goals* and *Three goals today! Francis scored them.*) The theme of 1 is the player, Francis, and the story tells what Francis did. The theme of 2 is *three goals*, and the story answers the question 'who scored them?' The change from active to passive, then, is not merely a repositioning of actors on the syntactic stage; it is in effect a change of plot. Compare the following two passages:

(1) A royal personage was to open a new wing of the cottage hospital, and all the villagers made efforts to ensure that her visit would be a memorable one. Bands of indefatigable Boy Scouts collected vast sums of money. Enthusiasts ran lotteries and bran tubs; there were flower shows and bingo sessions; benevolent pensioners performed prodigious feats of bowling and choral singing. Every able Jack and mobile Jill made a contribution.

(2) A new wing of the cottage hospital was to be opened by a royal personage, and great efforts were made by all the villagers to ensure that her visit would be a memor-

able one. Vast sums of money were collected by bands of indefatigable Boy Scouts. Lotteries and bran tubs were organized; flowers shows and bingo sessions were arranged; prodigious feats of bowling and choral singing were performed by benevolent pensioners. Contributions were made by every able Jack and mobile Jill.

Though they use the same material, there is in these passages a contrasting scheme of prominences. Example 1 is about *agents* choosing and controlling their activities; example 2 describes *activities* drawing agents into their train – a turnabout which creates a slightly different narrative.

In some varieties of technical prose, e.g. the language of scientific report, the passive is a regular and conventional feature. Elsewhere it is the marked form contrasting with the 'norm' of the active. Use it –

(a) In narrative or in rhetorical prose, to give chosen elements the prominence of 'fronting'.
(b) To disclaim agency; to make detached or impersonal statements, particularly in report. The form of the passive which deletes the '*by*-phrase' is often used in this way. (*A measure will shortly be introduced*; *The proposal has been considered*.)
(c) To adjust the rhythm and weight of a sentence – e.g. to correct 'front-heaviness': *A public anxiously mindful of the toll of lives in the Chicago air disaster raised objections* may be recast as *Objections were raised by a public anxiously mindful of the toll of lives in the Chicago air disaster*.
(d) As one of the means by which transitions from clause to clause or sentence to sentence may be facilitated. The passive transformation puts an adverbial phrase or the verb itself into the end-position, and this sometimes makes a convenient antecedent base: *A fine sermon was preached by the bishop* ↔ *who later entertained us with a harmonica recital*; *A clinic equipped with the most advanced facilities for the treatment of sick children was today officially opened by the Princess of Wales.* ↔ *Her Royal Highness visited the wards, and spent some time with the young inmates*. In the first

of these examples, a noun is immediately followed by its relative pronoun; in the second, a noun phrase and its synonymic variant are placed next to each other.

## Option 7 *'Declarative' versus 'postpositive' sentence forms*

The 'declarative' construction simply makes a statement about a theme. What is here called the 'postpositive' type of construction (i.e. the existential sentence, the extraposition, the cleft sentence – see 2.9) puts the theme, or a whole statement, into end-focus.
Examples:

(1a) His failure is evident. ('Declarative')
(1b) It is evident that he has failed. ('Postpositive')

(2a) Problems abounded. ('Declarative')
(2b) There were abundant problems. ('Postpositive')

(3a) Eve stole the apple. ('Declarative')
(3b) It was Eve who stole the apple. ('Postpositive')

Comment:

Example 1b is an *extraposition*, 2b is an *existential sentence*, and 3b is a *cleft sentence*. What they have in common is the use of a formulaic device (*it is*, *there are*, etc.) which is the verbal marker of an ensuing statement. (For fuller comment, see 2.9.) The forms give notice of an intention to state, or announce the performance of stating, and in that way may seem somewhat detached, academic, artificial. This is an impression which a little attention to everyday conversational exchanges may well challenge. *It's plain to anyone that he's on the make*, *There's a maggot in that lettuce*, *It's you that need a psychiatrist* are no more 'artificial' than *His aspirations are clear to all*, *That lettuce contains a maggot*, and *The person who needs a psychiatrist is you*. In many cases the postpositive form is the natural turn of speech. (*There's a knife in that drawer* is 'unmarked' by comparison with *A knife is in that drawer* or even *A knife will be found in that drawer*.)

Nevertheless, a common effect of 'postposing' is to put objects at a cool, impersonal distance, and often to draw the rough energy out of a text. Compare two versions of a narrative:

(1) Everyone had obviously been looking forward to the team's return. Expectancy hung in the air; groups of people lined the platform, sporting rosettes and scarves, or clutching home-made banners. For a while nobody spoke. Then the stationmaster broke the silence.

(2) It was obvious that everyone had been looking forward to the team's return. There was a general air of expectancy; all along the platform there were groups of people sporting rosettes and scarves or shouldering home-made banners. There was an interval when nobody spoke. It was the stationmaster who eventually broke the silence.

Version 2 suffers a little in the comparison. It lacks narrative urgency; in particular, the 'postpositive' forms greatly detract from the stylistic power of the verb. (Compare *there was a general air of expectancy* with *expectancy hung in the air*; *all along the platform there were groups of people* with *groups of people lined the platform*.) Narrative can certainly make effective use of postpositive structures – *Pride and Prejudice* begins with one – but seldom in the density suggested here. They are not uncommon in the prose of reasoning and analysis, where they can be used –

(a) To state a generalized, impersonal, 'objective' case: *It is agreed that prisons are expensive to maintain.*
(b) To express a verdict or judgment, as though with the weight of impartial authority: *There is no greater musician than Mozart.*
(c) To give a syntactic framework to a nominal item (phrase or clause), for the purpose of presenting it to a reader. Thus, to convey the notion *objections to this argument*, one may use the frame of an existential proposition, *There are objections to this argument*, which may be preferable to the front-weighted *Objections to this argument exist*, or the passive *Objections to this argument may be raised.*
(d) As one of the means of dealing with the recurrent problem of front-heaviness. Thus *Jack's habit of solving his problems partly by resorting to the bottle and partly by sheer self-deception is well known* is an awkwardly-

balanced construction that might be more effectively poised in an extraposition: *It is well known that Jack is in the habit of solving his problems partly by resorting to the bottle and partly by sheer self-deception.*

## 4 Options of address

Seldom is writing wholly a matter of expounding facts clearly and objectively, without reference to personal attitudes and relationships. There is, to be sure, a stylistic discretion, recommended in 3.5, but even within that neutral pale there may be manifestations of personality and attitude. As a style extends its ambitions, these manifestations are more frequent and more complex. Many writings represent a blending, whether skilful and deliberate or merely haphazard, of a 'speech-style' that echoes the informalities of ordinary conversation, and a 'book-style' reflecting the artifice and formality of literary convention.

'Book-style' is not necessarily equated with the idiom of literary art. It refers to a general mode of address incorporating features found in relatively high density in formal writing and somewhat lower density in informal daily talk; 'speech-style' characterizes elements in language strongly associated with personal interaction. Below are listed some prominent features of the two modes. The tendency, in written communications, for formal to merge into informal must be kept in mind. Further, we should take note of the artifice and occasional stiltedness of some bookish devices; the fact that they are mentioned here does not amount to a recommendation for use. For that a context is required, and some knowledge of the user's intention.

| *Speech-style* | *Book-style* |
|---|---|
| Use of personal pronouns, *I, we, you*; *I will give an example*; *We shall see*; *You should take care*. | Avoidance of personal pronouns; compensatory use of passives and postpositive forms: *An example may be given*; *It will become apparent*; *Care should be taken*. |

| Speech-style | Book-style |
|---|---|
| Use of contracted forms, e.g. *they've, there'd, we're, answer's.* | Preference for expanded forms, e.g. *they have, there would, we are, answer is.* |
| General preference for 'non-modal' assertions: *I think he was foolish to leave; You win; You'll find it in any decent grammar.* | Recourse to the speculation and ironic formality of 'modal' constructions: *I would have thought his departure ill-considered; It might appear that the victory is yours; Readers may care to consult a reliable grammer.* |
| | (About the examples, note (a) that the modals occur in conjunction with other style-features, and (b) that this kind of wordiness, even with the best of facetious intentions, irritates many people). |
| Somewhat restricted use of postpositive structures (but see the comment on Option 7). | Relatively frequent use of postpositive structures, notably in expository and analytical prose. |
| Preference for the positive and the overstated: *They are clever; The plan is sure to fail.* | Frequent use of the negative and the understated: *They are not unskilled; The plan is hardly assured of success.* |
| | (Note: In British usage, ironic modality, negation, and understatement may often be interpreted as marks of class — symptoms of 'talking posh'). |
| Use of exclamations and direct questions: *How strange!; What is the solution?* | Avoidance (by periphrasis, by the use of adverbial intensifiers, etc.) of the exclamatory and interrogative: *This is extraordinarily strange; A solution is called for.* |

## Options

| Speech-style | Book-style |
|---|---|
| Reliance on a 'coarse-graded' vocabulary, i.e. one with a low differentiation of synonyms; for example, *think, feel* to cover all manner of mental events. | Reliance on a 'fine-graded' vocabulary, i.e. one with a high differentiation of synonyms: *think, feel, suppose, consider, conjecture, estimate, assume, infer, surmise, suspect, speculate,* etc. |
| Use of a 'free' vocabulary – i.e. free from constraints of text type or social propriety: *The guests enjoyed the affair/'do'/beano/get-together.* Attendant vice: laxity of expression. | Use of a 'bound' vocabulary – i.e. dictated by text-type and social constraints: Jack's *party* is Jill's *reception* is a memorable *occasion* is a ceremonial *banquet* is a distinguished *assembly* is an informal *gathering.* Attendant vice: fixity of expression, i.e. cliché. |

Texts present these elements in various mixtures. We may consequently speak of a *level of address* in assessing the extent to which features of speech-style or book-style predominate. In some texts the level of address remains fairly constant throughout; in others, for example in polemic and in some types of humour, there may be frequent shifts of level.

This is a complex topic, difficult to handle briefly, even more difficult to reduce to terms of serviceable recommendation. The two options briefly and rather tentatively set out below are of a general nature. One concerns the writer's attitude to his reader – his facial expression, as it were, or tone of voice; the other is a matter of grooming the text, to make a crisply assertive showing or to present a more circumstantial style.

### Option 8 *Informal/familiar versus formal/convential*

The labels speak for themselves; they denote the effect of language in bringing the writer closer to the reader, with a sense of intimacy, warmth, ordinariness, etc., or setting him at a distance in polite reserve and social convention. Attempts at the latter often result in the pompous wordiness

illustrated by one or two of the following examples:
Examples (a):

(1) The chairman and the treasurer voted for cuts.

(2) It was felt by the chairman and the treasurer that economies would be in order.

Comment:
Sentence 1 puts its message in familiar style; sentence 2 somewhat laboriously keeps the matter at a distance. The means of 'distancing' are (i) the postpositive construction (*It was the case X that clause Y*) (ii) the passive (*was felt by*), (iii) the use of the modal *would be* (rather than *were*), plus a 'book-style' cliché *be in order*, and (iv) the 'bound' element in the vocabulary (*economies* is conventionally appropriate to the language of official report, and to the institutional pomp of the chairman and treasurer).
Examples (b):

(1) If you dissociate the study of speech from its proper connection with the study of creativeness in language, you allow it to become a mere adjunct of genteel nurture, like social etiquette or discreet tailoring. You make a word a blow to self-esteem; you let a man's vowels decide whether he is fit to hold a commission.

(2) To dissociate the study of speech from its proper connection with the study of creativeness in language is to allow it to become a mere adjunct of genteel nurture, like etiquette or discreet tailoring. A word becomes a blow to self-esteem; a man's vowels are allowed to decide whether he is fit to hold a commission.

Comment:
The significant difference between these examples is that in sentence 2 the pronoun *you* is replaced by constructions which avoid personality. The infinitive, the passive, the inanimate subject, are used to keep *you* at a distance. Though the alteration in wording is quite small, the contrast is striking. Note particularly the treatment of the first sentence in the two versions. In 1 the opening sentence is introduced by a left-branching subordinate clause (*If you dissociate . . . language*).

The corresponding sentence in version 2 has no branching, but consists of a single clause with elaborate embeddings; S is an infinitive clause (*to dissociate . . . language*), and C another infinitive with yet a third infinitive embedded in it (*to allow it to become a mere adjunct of genteel nurture*). In this instance, the process of 'depersonalizing' radically affects the syntax.

(1) The food's marvellous, though the rooms aren't all that good.

(2) The cuisine is deserving of the highest praise; the accommodation, however, leaves something to be desired.

Comment:
The context evoked here is that of commending a hotel, resort, etc., whether privately, as in a letter, or more publicly, as in the columns of a journal, or in some form of official report. In sentence 1 the marks of informality are obvious: the contractions (*food's, aren't*), the freely coarse-graded word (*marvellous*), the colloquial intensifier (*all that* in *all that good*). In sentence 2 there are 'bound' elements, *cuisine* and *accommodation*, clearly dictated by the etiquette of this type of discourse. (*Rooms* are conventionally *accommodation*, and *cuisine* has a social and professional advantage over mere *cooking*.) In addition there are clichés, also bound to the convention, and absurdly stiff in their bindings: *deserving of the highest praise, leaves something to be desired*.

Examples (d):

(1) The book is rather dull.

(2) The book could hardly be called sparkling.

(3) The author is learned, sincere, painstaking, but unimaginative.

(4) The author is not without learning, and lacks neither sincerity nor the capacity for taking pains; his defect is a want of imagination.

Comment:
As a rule, assertion by negatives is a bad stylistic habit; sentences 1 and 3 have the merit of coming directly to the

point. Sometimes, however, a bantering and ironic detachment may be expressed through negation and other devices – e.g. the adverb suggesting a negative evaluation (*hardly*), or the verb or noun denoting a negative concept (*lacks*, *defect*, *want*). The examples point to the verbose habit of the negating and understating style; its banter is often ponderous. These sentences also suggest how an elaborate formality of style may necessarily combine several features – e.g. in sentence 2, the understatement of *hardly*, the modality of *could*, the passive of *be called*, and the fine-graded choice of word in *sparkling*.

Option 9 *Pattern versus paraphrase*

The art of rhetoric includes many figures of speech that require symmetrical balances, antitheses, repetitions and parallels in the structure of phrases, clauses and sentences. There is an artistic patterning of language that occurs not only in literary texts, but also in diverse non-literary functions, and in everyday talk. Its counterpart is a dutiful discursiveness that chooses to paraphrase or 'spell out' a meaning rather than reduce its expression to a compact pattern.
Examples:

(1) Waste not, want not.

(2) If you avoid waste, you will never be in need.

(3) By making even the most trivial savings now, you may be ensuring survival and prosperity at some later date.

(4) Argyle make friends but Watford make history. (headline in *The Times*)

(5) Argyle pleased the spectators with courageous and skilful play, but it was Watford who, for the first time, won a place in the Cup Final.

Comment:
Examples 1 and 4 are patterned (with *w* echoing *w*, *waste* matched by *want*, *make* repeated in a variation of meaning) and have the pithiness that so often characterizes patterned utterance. There is a kind of riddling in them, an air of things unsaid that intelligence or experience must supply. Examples 2, 3, and 5 run to some length in their attempt to spell out a

meaning, leaving nothing to conjecture. Sentences 2 and 3 are in effect explanations of sentence 1, 3 being the fuller (or fussier) interpretation. Sentence 5 expounds the headline message of sentence 4. The examples conveniently illustrate by mutual reference the notions of pattern and paraphrase. There may be times when we experiment with a pattern and reject it in favour of a paraphrase, or begin a paraphrase only to realize that the intended meaning might be more cogently expressed through a pattern.

The multiplicity of verbal patterns can be reduced to three powerful configurations, often picked out by alliteration or some other phonetic device: the parallel, or yoke, the antithesis, or cross, and the sequence, or chain.
Examples:

(1) Man proposes, God disposes.

(Thomas à Kempis)

(2) One must eat to live, not live to eat.

(Molière)

(3) . . . and that government of the people, by the people, for the people, shall not perish from the earth.

(Abraham Lincoln)

Comment:
These classic examples illustrate, in the first instance, an arrangement of parallel clauses; in the second, an antithetical balance (the example presents the figure technically known as *antimetabole*, or *chiasmus*), and in the third place, a cumulative sequence of noun phrases marked by the evidently accented prepositions ('*of* the people, *by* the people, and *for* the people'). The ingenuity of these simple compressive patterns is soon discovered if one attempts to paraphrase them, e.g.: *Humanity has many aspirations and projects, but they are all subject to the will of God*; *Although eating keeps us alive, it is not the chief purpose of living*. Often it seems easier to make a pattern than to attempt a paraphrase, e.g. to say *The longer he lives the less he learns* rather than *His capacity to*

*learn from experience seems if anything to decrease with the passage of time.*

In general, patterning compresses, paraphrase expands. At times, however, a pattern may appear to be a form of carefully designed expansion. Compare, for instance:

> . . . that democracy shall not die

with

> . . . that government of the people, by the people, and for the people, shall not perish from the earth.

The latter may in its turn be paraphrased expansively:

> . . . that a political system allowing all citizens an equal share in the government of their country shall not become obsolete.

Lincoln's rhetoric takes a middle course (and a supremely effective one) between a laconic compression and a windy expansion.

Two passages of prose, one a classic text, the other by a famous authority on language and style, may be used to illustrate this contrast of patterning and paraphrase. The first is from Bacon's essay 'Of Studies':

> Reading maketh a full man; conference, a ready man; and writing an exact man. And therefore, if a man write little, he had need have a great memory; if he confer little, he had need have a present wit; and if he read little, he had need have much cunning, to seem to know that he doth not.

The author of the second passage is Samuel Johnson, writing at something less than his formidable best:

> The graces of writing and conversation are of different kinds, and though he who excels in one might have been with opportunities and application equally successful in the other, yet as many please by extemporary talk, though utterly unacquainted with the more accurate method, and more laboured beauties, which composition requires; so it is very possible that men, wholly accustomed to works of study, may be without that readiness of conception, and affluence of language, always necessary to colloquial enter-

tainment. They may want address to watch the hints which conversation offers for the display of their particular attainments, or they may be so much unfurnished with matter on common subjects, that discourse not professedly literary glides over them . . .
(*The Rambler*, no.14, 5 May 1750)

These two excerpts are comparable in content. Each is concerned with the various skills of language, and each points out that an individual may be practised in one skill and less adept in another. Bacon tells us what reading, writing, and discussion (*conference*) will severally do for us, and what compensatory powers we might need should we be defective in any of these. Johnson tells us that although some people may be equally skilled in writing and talking, there are many good talkers who cannot write well, and many practised writers who are poor conversationalists. His theme reflects that of Bacon. There are even points of verbal resemblance. Bacon's *a ready man* has its counterpart in Johnson's *readiness of conception, and affluence of language*; Johnson's *more accurate method . . . which composition requires* suggests Bacon's *an exact man*.

Where the two passages differ wholly is in their stylistic method. Bacon patterns his observations, reducing them to the memorable concision of maxims or proverbs. There are two sentences in the quoted excerpt, and each is built on a scheme of parallels. (Note how the sequence of key items in the second sentence reverses that of the first: (1) *Reading . . . conference . . . writing*; (2) *write . . . confer . . . read . . .* ). This powerful brevity is exhilarating. It raises, however, certain problems of definition. We are left to supply our own interpretation of several words of large import, e.g. *full, ready, exact*. Bacon sets us the task of analysing his lexicon. What does he mean by *ready* – quick to respond, fluent, quick-witted, astute? Or by *exact* –precise in exposition, accurate in recollection? The price of compression is a measure of obscurity.

There is no jauntily helpful patterning in the second passage. The modern reader may need a gloss on the syntax, which is constructed round the bracketing expression *as . . . so*; 'Yet just as there are many who please by casual talk, though they have no skill in writing, so it is possible that scholars and men of letters may be dull conversationalists.' The writing answers to our term *paraphrase*, in its evident attempt to explain, analyse and define. Some expressions wear an eighteenth-century look (*extemporary, laboured beauties, address, unfurnished*), but there are no problem words that tease the reader with their uncertain breadth of implication. Everything is spelt out, a symptom of this being the recurrent coordination of nouns and noun phrases: *opportunities and application; the more accurute method, and more laboured beauties; that readiness of conception, and affluence of language.* The 'spelling out' almost erodes the sense of the passage, and careful definition extends to the verge of incoherence.

Despite the defects of this particular excerpt (in sharp contrast with the merits of Bacon's text), its paraphrase technique does represent a norm, or staple, of prose exposition. Bacon's terse patterns suit the conception of his *Essays*, which treat their themes in summary and synoptic fashion. Two or three pages of this trimmed and dapper style are delightful, and it is invaluable for crystallizing a thought or caging a wayward insight; but for long excursions into complicated topics we need a more prolix habit, with sentences constructed to define, explain, amplify and qualify. In the long run we have more to say than epigrams and aphorisms will manage for us. We have tales to unfold. Now here is a further theme, for the unfolding calls for devices to control the expansion of the text and keep its meaning clear; and among these devices, the resources of punctuation are supremely important.

# 5
# Punctuations

> This fellow doth not stand upon points.
> — Theseus, in *A Midsummer Night's Dream*

> So now, my solemn ones, leaving the rest unsaid,
> Rising in air as on a gander's wings
> At a careless comma,
> —Robert Graves

### 1 Punctuation as a creative principle

Schoolroom practice encourages the assumption that punctuation is a corrective and editorial act, the particulars of which are worked out after a piece of writing has been drafted. This is at best an incomplete view of the matter. To punctuate is an integral part of the developing process of composition; as we choose words, as we conceive the pattern of the text, so we evolve designs in punctuation. There may certainly be a phase of revision, when oversights are corrected, ambiguities resolved, relationships clarified; in essence, however, punctuation is a creative act, and its options are bound up with other textual options.

This theme is admirably illustrated by the scrupulous and elegant patterning of Evelyn Waugh's prose, in his life of the Jesuit priest and martyr Edmund Campion. The book is a stylistic model deserving of the most detailed study. Here is a part of its opening paragraph:

> In the middle of March 1603 it was clear to everyone that Queen Elizabeth was dying; her doctors were unable to diagnose the illness; she had little fever, but was constantly thirsty, restless and morose; she refused to take medicine,

refused to eat, refused to go to bed. She sat on the floor, propped up with cushions, sleepless and silent, her eyes constantly open, fixed on the ground, oblivious to the coming and going of her councillors and attendants. She had done nothing to recognize her successor; she had made no provision for the disposal of her property, of the vast, heterogeneous accumulation of a lifetime, in which presents had come to her daily from all parts of the world; closets and cupboards stacked high with jewellery, coin, bric-a-brac; the wardrobe of two thousand outmoded dresses. There was always company in the little withdrawing room waiting for her to speak, but she sighed and sipped and kept her silence.

The reader must immediately notice how semi-colons mark the construction of this piece of text. The articulation and phrasing of the passage, its very rhythm, seem to require them. But the semi-colon is only one element in a design that requires another mark of punctuation, the comma. We might say that two 'styles' of punctuation, a 'semi-colon style' and a 'comma style', here alternate and blend. Thus, the passage begins with a sentence in which a textual relationship is imposed on four constituent sentences, separated yet linked by semi-colons:

> In the middle of March 1603 it was clear to everyone that Queen Elizabeth was dying; her doctors were unable to diagnose her illness; she had little fever, but was constantly thirsty, restless and morose; she refused to take medicine, refused to eat, refused to go to bed.

The description 'separated yet linked', an apparent contradiction in terms, expresses a signal characteristic of this mark of punctuation; it disjoins one syntactic unit from the next, yet implies a relationship between the two. Compare this with the wholly disjunctive effect of full stops:

> In the middle of March 1603 it was clear to everyone that Queen Elizabeth was dying. Her doctors were unable to diagnose the illness. She had little fever, but was constantly thirsty, restless and morose. She refused to take medicine, refused to eat, refused to go to bed.

This rewriting suggests a different sort of distributive option (see 4.2). The movement from stop to stop suggests a list, whereas the semi-colons of the original present something more like a continuous expansion of the opening statement. Correspondingly, there are implied differences of tempo, rhythm, and intonation.

In the next sentence it is the comma that assumes the creative, pattern-giving role:

> She sat on the floor, propped up with cushions, sleepless and silent, her eyes constantly open, fixed on the ground, oblivious to the coming and going of her councillors and attendants.

Syntactically, this sentence is a sequence of non-finite (participle or verbless) clauses, linked recursively by commas to the main clause with which the sentence opens. All but one of the elements in this array depend on the subject *She*:

```
   ┌She ... sat ... on the floor
   │ └propped up with cushions
   │  └sleepless and silent
   │   └her eyes constantly open
   └oblivious to the coming
    and going of her council-
    lors and attendants.
```

The odd element, not represented in the diagram above, is the participle clause *fixed on the ground*. This alone does not depend on *she*; it is governed by *eyes* in the immediately preceding clause, and the momentary change of government is perhaps disturbing at first glance, because it invites the reader to relate *oblivious* to the same antecedent, *eyes*: 'her eyes (were) constantly open, (were) fixed on the ground, (were) oblivious to the coming and going of her councillors'. The meaning of the word itself tells us that *oblivious* cannot depend on *eyes*, and that the reference has shifted back to *she*. The casual displacement in the syntax is a departure from the habitual accuracy of Waugh's style, and creates a minor confusion which might have been removed simply by writing *her eyes constantly fixed on the ground* without adding the unnecessary information that these 'fixed' eyes were 'open'.

This is a cavil, however, and an incidental reminder that we may discover lapses of construction in the most brilliant writings. The error (if that is the right word) is induced by the pull of the dominant structural force. Here we have a sentence in which the organizing agent is the comma, not the semi-colon. A semi-colon pattern, or a combination of semi-colons and commas, would be possible:

> She sat on the floor, propped up with cushions; sleepless and silent; her eyes constantly open, fixed on the ground; oblivious to the coming and going of her attendants and councillors.

This is an interesting arrangement, but one that repeats the design principle of the first sentence. In Waugh's conception there is a stylistic change from government by semi-colons to a pattern turning on commas.

The third sentence reintroduces the semi-colon as the major item of punctuation:

> She had done nothing to recognize her successor; she had made no provision for the disposal of her property, of the vast, heterogeneous accumulation of a lifetime, in which presents had come to her daily from all parts of the world; closets and cupboards stacked high with jewellery, coin, bric-a-brac; the wardrobe of two thousand outmoded dresses.

Here the semi-colon is used to signal two different types of relationship. In its first occurrence, its role is the usual one of disjoining grammatically independent yet topically linked elements: *She had done nothing to recognize her successor*; *she had made no provisions for the disposal of her property*. The semi-colons after *world* and *bric-a-brac* are operators of another kind. They are exemplifiers, denoting 'for instance', marking the citation of particulars, indicating the dependence of the ensuing text on some preceding element. In this case the 'preceding element' is the word *accumulation*:

accumulation (e.g.)    (i) closets and cupboards stacked high with jewellery etc.

                                  (ii) the wardrobe of two thousand outmoded dresses

There is a stylistic complication, therefore, in the development of this sentence. The semi-colons have their customary function of marking out expository segments, in this case enclosing a rather long second component (*she had made no provision*, etc.), a right-branching clause running to thirty-three words. This is the central mass of the text, and round it the signposting semi-colons point in different directions. The first semi-colon suggests a pointing forward (*she had done nothing* → *she had made no provision*), while the second and third invite backward reference (from *closets and cupboards*, etc., to *accumulation*).Thus there is a skilfully contrived inward-pointing, from either end of the sentence to its long central construction:

she had *done nothing* → she had *made no provision* for the disposal of her property, of the vast *accumulation* ← *closets and cupboards*, etc.
*the wardrobe*, etc.

The fourth sentence returns to the rule of the comma, but introduces a new and interesting option:

There was always company in the little withdrawing room waiting for her to speak, but she sighed and sipped and kept her silence.

The comma and the contrastive *but* mark the coordination of two major structural blocks. It is in the second of these blocks (*she sighed and sipped*, etc.) that the new option appears, presenting a choice between the comma and *zero* – i.e. the absence of any mark of punctuation:

*comma*: she sighed, and sipped, and kept her silence

*zero*: she sighed and sipped and kept her silence

In this case the presence or absence of punctuation will not affect the sense of the construction, but must certainly modify its expressiveness, much as the presence or absence of dynamic marks in music will affect phrasing in performance. A rhythm, a tempo, a pattern of intonation, even a way of looking at events, may be suggested.

This analysis of punctuation in a few lines of highly accomplished prose rests on the assumption (a) that there is a discernible pattern, involving the selection and alternation of devices, and (b) that punctuation is 'conceived', along with other stylistic elements with which it enters into play. The assumption appears to be justified by the textual facts. In particular, our model text would seem to suggest a relationship between the problems and options of distribution (see 4.2) and sets of choices in punctuation, e.g.:

full stop versus semi-colon:

> She had done nothing to recognize her successor. She had made no provision for the disposal of her property

or

> She had done nothing to recognize her successor; she had made no provision for the disposal of her property.

semi-colon versus comma:

> She refused to take medicine; she declined food; she could not be persuaded to go to bed

or

> She refused to take medicine, refused to eat, refused to go to bed.

comma versus zero:

> She sighed, and sipped, and kept her silence

or

> She sighed and sipped and kept her silence.

These rudimentary options can be compounded in various ways, e.g.:

full stop versus semi-colon and comma:

> She sat sleepless and silent on the floor. Her eyes were constantly open and fixed on the ground. She was oblivious to the coming and going of her attendants

or

> She sat on the floor, sleepless and silent; her eyes constantly open, fixed on the ground; oblivious to the coming and going of her attendants.

semi-colon and comma versus comma:

> She had little fever, but was constantly thirsty, restless and morose; she refused to take medicine, refused to eat, refused to go to bed

or

> She had little fever, but was constantly thirsty, restless, morose, refusing to take medicine, refusing to eat, refusing to go to bed.

To devise further examples would be an exercise in permutation that perhaps may be omitted. It appears that there is a system of *stops* providing options for thoughtful composition. In these options other choices are implied; some of the examples above show variations in grammatical structure and in vocabulary. In some cases the mark of punctuation is apparently the sole connection between juxtaposed constructions, while in others the linkage is additionally marked by some grammatical connective. A further instance:

> (a) In the middle of March 1603 it was clear to everyone that Queen Elizabeth was dying; her doctors were unable to diagnose the illness.
>
> The semi-colon is the organizing mark of relationship between the two clauses. (Though not the sole connective; *her* makes linking reference to *Queen Elizabeth*). The method of organization leaves the reader free to interpret the status of the second clause, i.e. to decide whether it depends on the first, and if so how (= 'although'? = 'nevertheless'? = 'however'?).
>
> (b) In the middle of March 1603 it was clear to everyone that Queen Elizabeth was dying, although her doctors were unable to diagnose the illness.

The comma marks off the clauses, but the primary connective is the conjunction *although*. This imposes a reading, by clearly relegating the second clause to a subordinate status in which it expresses a concession or qualification.

In the second of these versions, punctuation is used to mark and support an explicitly stated grammatical relationship. This is perhaps how we commonly see its function; as a syntactic auxiliary. In the first version, however, punctuation assumes the main connective role. Here is a valuable stylistic alternative, offering an occasional escape from the routine harness of *and, but, although, furthermore, namely*, etc.

## 2 Marks of sense, marks of expression

Punctuation is used to convey two kinds of message. It tells the reader about the grouping and connection of syntactic elements, so that he can properly interpret a meaning without falling foul of ambiguities and false relationships. In addition, it presents the score of a vocal performance; it notates, albeit in a rather limited way, details of tempo, rhythm and inflection, projecting a tone of voice and an attitude which the reader, if he is skilled and sensitive, can diagnose. Punctuation, in short, makes *sense* and projects *attitudes*.

In literary composition these functions often overlap, and are necessarily discharged by the same symbols; a grammatically obligatory comma may also mark a pause or an intonation. This duplicity complicates the analysis of punctuation, and it may therefore be useful to consider one or two examples, firstly of punctuating for sense and secondly of scoring an attitude.

*Making sense*

Example A:

(i) He was certain that the injured man had died long before the doctor arrived.

(ii) He was certain that the injured man had died, long before the doctor arrived.

Comment;
The problem is to define the antecedent of *long before*. A

version i with zero punctuation leaves the reader to assume that *died* is the word on which the final clause depends (*the man died long before the doctor arrived*). The comma of version ii purportedly shifts the reference back to *certain* (*he was certain long before the doctor arrived*). Such a shift could be more clearly indicated by moving the problem element from its end-position to a place immediately after *certain*, where commas would be optional: *He was certain* [,] *long before the doctor arrived* [,] *that the injured man had died.*

Example B:

(i) The councillors who have taken a stand against the Minister's recommendation were today dismissed from office.

(ii) The councillors, who have taken a stand against the Minister's recommendations, were today dismissed from office.

Comment:
The two versions represent the distinction between relative clauses in so-called 'restrictive' and 'non-restrictive' applications. In version i the reference is specifically to certain councillors, by implication excluding others. In version ii there is no such restrictive or specifying intention; the clause between commas adds a piece of information relating to councillors generally, and does not specify some to the exclusion of the rest.

*Projecting attitudes*

Example A:

(i) He was certain that his entry had succeeded – long before the confirmatory telegram arrived!

Comment:
Here is a copywriter's device: the enthusiastic coupling of dash and exclamation point. The dash after *succeeded* makes sense as securely as any comma, relating *long before* to *certain*. This, however, is a secondary intention. The primary role of the dash is to 'score' a style of performance, suggesting, perhaps, the dramatic hiatus, the emphatic falling pitch on *long*, the intonation that assertively forestalls objection or

disbelief. For this dramatizing purpose, the dash works in tandem with the mark of exclamation.

Example B:

(i) She left the web . . . left the loom . . . crossed to the window in three paces; looked out; saw Lancelot (magnificent in full armour) riding by – and made her way briskly to the boathouse.

Comment:
A small repertoire of gestures is involved in this punctuational drama. Tennyson contented himself with commas in the original: *She left the web, she left the loom, she made three paces through the room.* The dots and the abrupt dash can be read partly as marks of tempo, partly as stage directions (so to speak), partly as extravagant mimetic signals, like the broad actions of a 'ham' actor. The semi-colons are notations of timing (compare the given version with an alternative possibility, *crossed to the window in three paces, looked out, saw Lancelot*). A further note for performance is registered by the brackets round *magnificent in full armour*. They score a change in vocal pitch and loudness, implying the dropped note, the levelled intonation, the reduction to murmur-volume.

These examples illustrate some of the ways in which punctuation may be used, on the one hand as a guide to textual relationships, and on the other as notation representing a style of vocal delivery. For further discussion and illustration, we need to consider marks of punctuation under three heads:

(a) *stops*, or marks of separation

(b) *suspensions*, i.e. marks of interruption, apposition or citation

(c) *scorings*, or marks of expression

### 3 Stops

There is a great subtlety, and for the writer great technical interest, in the process of putting down marks that identify and precisely interconnect the constituents of a sentence or a text. The repertoire includes the full stop, the colon, the semi-colon, the comma, and – if an omission can be reckoned a device – a calculated avoidance of stops, our so-called 'zero punctuation'.

(i) *The full stop*

The full stop is conveniently defined as the mark that indicates the end of a sentence:

> The day was very hot. The house looked invitingly cool. I went in.

The simple sentences in this example, however, might be separated by semi-colons:

> The day was very hot; the house looked invitingly cool; I went in.

or even by commas:

> The day was very hot, the house looked invitingly cool, I went in.

There are in fact many contexts in which the full stop and the semi-colon, in particular, can be regarded as alternative forms of stopping.

One criterion of choice between them is the assumption of connectedness. A semi-colon invites the reader to construct lines of relationship in the most unlikely juxtapositions. Here is a random invention:

> Mr Smith takes a half day off every Wednesday; bread without jam is very dull.

The association between these two statements may apparently be tenuous to the point of non-existence, but the semi-colon linking them commands the reader to search for a design. It is strange how we respond instinctively to this command; there is in all of us a remarkable willingness to ascribe sense to any piece of connected text. In this case, the second statement might be read as a figurative comment on the first: Mr Smith's half day off is the jam on his routine bread. The conjecture has only to be made for the reader to grasp at it, convinced of its rightness. His readiness to make assumptions is much weaker when the two statements are separated by a full stop:

> Mr Smith takes a half day off every Wednesday. Bread without jam is very dull.

The suggested interpretation may still be made (especially if prompted by hints from a wider context) but a sensitive writer must now feel the compulsion to devise some overt verbal link between the sentences:

> Mr Smith takes a half day off every Wednesday. Bread without jam, after all, is very dull.

Here *after all* prompts the reader to make the desired figurative connection.

One short passage will serve to illustrate the stylistic value of the full stop in relation to the syntactic patterning, the dynamics of expression, and the general level of address (see 4.4) in a text. It is from Jerome K. Jerome's humorous classic *Three Men in a Boat*:

> Then I wondered how long I had to live. I tried to examine myself. I felt my pulse. I could not at first feel any pulse at all. Then, all of a sudden, it seemed to start off. I pulled out my watch and timed it. I made it a hundred and forty seven to the minute. I tried to feel my heart. I could not feel my heart. It had stopped beating.

Jerome here takes the distributive option (see 4.2) of constructing a sequence of short sentences. We are consequently aware of the full stop as the dominant mark of punctuation. The comic effectiveness of his choice can be assessed by 'redistributing' the content of the passage, making use of the comma as linking device:

> Then, wondering how long I had to live, I tried to examine myself. My pulse at first could not be felt, but all of a sudden it seemed to begin and I took out my watch to time it, noting a rate of a hundred and forty seven to the minute. When I tried to feel my heart, I could not do so; it had stopped beating.

This makes a fluent reading, but one that smoothes away the original's hopalong humour. The change has involved more than punctuation; syntax and wording have also been modified. In these comma-linked structures, the comic repetitions of *try, feel, pulse, heart,* have been lost. Subordinate clauses enter the pattern (e.g. *wondering how long I had to live*) and there is a variation of presentative emphasis (e.g. the use of the passive in *My pulse at first could not be felt*). In writing, one option keeps intricate company with others.

(ii) *The colon*

The colon doubles as a stop and as a mark of citation (see section 4 below). As a stop, it is commonly used –

(a) With the force of 'that is', 'namely', 'to wit', etc., in identifying a case or condition:

> Let us be clear about one thing: we have yet to solve our economic problems.

(b) To mark a powerful contrast or rhetorical counterpoise:

> Men create the problems: women suffer the consequences.

(c) To announce a conclusion:

> After years of trying to write stories I was obliged to face the truth: I had no talent.

(d) Pointedly to suggest cause or result:

> She could never leave him: she lacked the courage.
> (= 'because')

> He bought a very fast car: it killed him.
> (= 'the result was')

A subtler example of this causative/resultative use of the colon is provided in the closing sentences of James Joyce's short story 'A Painful Case':

> He waited for some minutes listening. He could hear nothing: the night was perfectly silent. He listened again: perfectly silent. He felt that he was alone.

The punctuation is almost symbolic, suggesting the rapt attentiveness of the listening man. The connective function of the colons veers between the 'causative' and the 'resultative'. The man can hear nothing *because* the night is silent; when he listens again (note how *listen* is the active counterpart of *hear*), the effort of listening produces no *result*. What the colons mark is a kind of turnabout between action and reaction, fact and explanation, process and consequence.

(iii) *The semi-colon*

This is the master stop of literary prose. Its principal use (as we have seen) is in the separation of clauses and sentences bearing a close topical relationship to each other, like the A and B elements in the following example:

A ↔ B
She was dying; her doctors could not diagnose the disease.

The meanings implied by the semi-colon, in its couplings of an A with a B, may be summarized as follows:

(a) A = B. Reiteration, or equation; in b, the content of a is repeated or paraphrased:

He was notorious for his dealings with women; his sexual exploits were the talk of the cafés.

(b) A + B. Juxtaposition; A and B present different aspects of one developing topic:

She walked slowly to the window; the loom shattered.

Longer sequences (A + B + C, etc.) may be evolved in this way:

The boat rocked gently; the river was dark and placid; autumn softened the air; the heaviness of sleep came upon her.

(c) A < B. Expansion; B enlarges upon A:

The symphony began; music, irresistible music, heavenly in its power to heal and reconcile, filled the auditorium.

(d) A > B. Exemplification and inference; B gives details in illustration of A's general statement, or specifies something implied in A:

The boxes were crammed with jewels; diamonds, sapphires, rubies like plums, precious stones of every kind. (*Exemplification*)

Syntactic and expressive functions often overlap; the comma is therefore an ambivalent mark of punctuation. (*Inference*)

As colons are also used to cite and specify, a colon would be an acceptable alternative punctuation in the first of these examples. It would suggest, however, an inclusive inventory rather than a general exemplification; it has the force of *namely*, whereas the semi-colon implies *for example* (Compare *Every child has two parents: a father and a mother* with *Every child has fears; of the dark, of animals, of authority*). A symptom of the type of relationship illustrated in the second example is that the punctuation is often reinforced by connectives like *therefore, for instance, thus*.

(e) A ≠ B. Opposition and concession; A and B are converse statements, or one modifies the other concessively:

Dr Johnson loved cats; Boswell disliked them.

The proofs were read with care; even so, some errors were undetected.

The concessive relationship in examples of the second type is indicated by expressions like *even so, nevertheless, however*.

The semi-colon and the comma are often used in combination, to mark out divisions and sub-divisions of text:

To begin your painting, you will need a palette, for mixing; several brushes, some of hogshair, some of sable, perhaps some of nylon; tubes of paint, acrylic or oil, in black, white, and the primary colours; and, of course, a canvas or board, with an easel to stand it on.

This common technique of sectioning by semi-colons and sub-sectioning by commas becomes a sensitive and subtle craft in the hands of a writer like Hemingway:

And up in Sidney's rooms, the ones coming to ask for work when he was fighting, the ones to borrow money, the ones for an old shirt, a suit of clothes; all bullfighters, all well known somewhere at the hour of eating, all formally polite, all out of luck; the muletas folded and piled; the capes all folded flat; swords in the embossed leather cases; all in the armoire; muleta sticks are in the bottom drawer, suits hung in the trunk, cloth covered to protect the gold; my whisky in an earthen crock; Mercedes, bring the glasses; she says he had a fever all night long and only went out an hour ago. (*Death in the Afternoon*)

Bold licenses are taken here. The thread of syntactic consistency is repeatedly broken; the semi-colons are ties joining different types of construction – participle clauses, verbless clauses, noun phrases, fully predicated sentences (*muleta sticks are in the bottom drawer*), sentences of direct speech (*Mercedes, bring the glasses*), sentences of reported speech (*she says he had a fever all night*). No less bold is the filmic tracking from topic to topic: first the bullfighters, then the wardrobe of bullfighting equipment, then a fragment of conversation. The impressionistic technique – presenting the blendings and switchings of memory – might puzzle and irritate the reader, were it not for a strict framework of punctuation that both highlights and controls the style.

(iv) *The comma*

The comma is the busiest of the stops, and probably the most difficult to use effectively. Modern writers appear to use it less scrupulously, in obedience to rule, than their eighteenth- and nineteenth-century counterparts; quite often the phrasing of a text is left to the interpretative choice of the reader. We have perhaps lost something of a feeling for what is necessary and what is adequate. There are competing vices. One is a neurotic over-stopping, of the kind for which the *New Yorker*, under the editorship of Harold Ross, used to be famous. James Thurber tells us in his book *The Years with Ross* of 'the unending fuss and fret about commas', which, he says, originated in 'Ross's clarification complex'. He illustrates:

> Now and then, the weedy growth of that punctuation mark, spreading through the magazine like dandelions, was more than I could bear with Christian fortitude. I once sent Ross a few typed lines out of one of Wordsworth's Lucy poems, repunctuated after his exasperating fashion:

> She lived, alone, and few could know
> When Lucy ceased to be,
> But, she is in her grave, and, oh,
> The difference, to me.

Thurber has a delightful explanation for an editorially imposed comma in the sentence *After dinner, the men went into the living-room*. It was, he alleges, 'Ross's way of giving the men time to push back their chairs and stand up'.

The opposing vice is that of under-stopping. If Thurber could produce an effect of ludicrous fussiness by over-punctuating Wordsworth, we might retort with the uncouth style of a comma-less *Gettysburg Address*:

> The brave men living and dead who struggled here have consecrated it far above our power to add or detract. The world will little note nor long remember what we say here but it can never forget what they did here. It is for us the living rather to be dedicated to the work they have thus far so nobly advanced. . .

This may not place any serious obstacle in the way of understanding but it compares poorly with the original, which has commas round *living and dead* and after *here* in the first sentence; round *nor long remember* and after *here* in the second sentence; and round *the living* in the third sentence.

Among the connective uses of the comma, the following are to be noted:

(1) In word-series, i.e. lists of adjectives, adverbs, nouns or verbs, where no coordinating conjunction occurs:

> Majorie was withdrawn, taciturn, introspective.
>
> Patiently, scrupulously, untiringly, he sifted the evidence.
>
> Towers, spires, chimneys rose on the skyline.
>
> A good teacher must wish to communicate, inform, persuade.

No comma is written between the last of a series of adjectives and a following noun (*a beautiful, intelligent, affectionate girl*), and frequently there is no comma between the last of a series of nouns and a following verb (*towers, spires, chimneys rose on the skyline*). In the latter case there is, however, an expressive option. It is possible to indicate a phrasing by writing, for example, *jars, tins, pots, packages, tumbled out of the cupboard*. In such cases the disjunction between the list of nouns and the ensuing predication is often more heavily marked by a dash preceding an anaphoric pronoun: *Jars, tins, pots, packages – all came tumbling out of the cupboard.*

When items are linked by coordinating conjunctions, the comma is an expressive option:

On the skyline were towers and spires and chimneys.

Or

On the skyline were towers, and spires, and chimneys.

Frequently the last item in a list is introduced by a coordinating conjunction, before which the comma is optional. Optional status is indicated in these examples by the bracketed mark [,]:

The room was littered with journals, books, papers [,] and files.

When the final item is a phrase, the preceding comma appears to be less freely optional:

The room was littered with journals, books, papers, and dusty old files.

The room was littered with journals, books, papers, and files of various kinds.

In the last example, the reason for the comma is obvious: it resolves an ambiguity, i.e. *papers + files of various kinds* versus *papers-and-files of various kinds*.

(2) In phrase-series, following the same general principles:

Tom was a man of great courage, full of humour, extraordinarily patient, the perfect travelling companion.

When phrases are linked by conjunctions, the comma, as before, becomes an expressive option:

He took out of his trunk a pair of shoes [,] and an old hat [,] and an opera cloak.

A comma is usual before the final, coordinated item of an otherwise conjunctionless series. Such items are often phrases with embedded clauses, in which case the very weight of the construction calls for a balancing comma:

> He took from his trunk a pair of shoes, an old hat, and an opera cloak that appeared to have seen better days.

(3) In marking off appositions and adverbial disjuncts:

> The Leader of the Opposition, Mr Neil Kinnock, has addressed the Labour Party Conference today.
>
> His insurance broker, a prudent man, advised him to raise the premium.
>
> The weather, unfortunately for us, kept all the ferries in harbour.
>
> Strange to say, services were resumed next morning.

With certain parenthetical conjuncts, such as *therefore, consequently, nevertheless*, the enclosing commas are an expressive option:

> Britain is an island. Nevertheless [,] it is a part of Europe.

*But* when the conjunct comes at the end of the sentence, the comma is obligatory:

> Britain is an island. It is a part of Europe, nevertheless.

(4) With tag-phrases, e.g. the question-tags of speech-style and the explanatory/concessive tags of book-style:

> Voltaire wrote *Candide*, didn't he?
>
> Voltaire, I believe, wrote *Candide*.
>
> Voltaire was a disinfectant, so to speak.

(5) With enumerative expressions, e.g. *first, next, lastly*:

> First, the subject is unpopular; second, the lecture takes place at an inconvenient time.

(6) Round phrases of address or invocation:

> These words, my dears, came from the heart.

Consider your history, people of Britain, and be warned by it.

(7) In clause-series, where successive constructions share an antecedent subject, or where there is a reiteration of a clause-pattern:

He got out of bed, pulled on his trousers, lurched to the door [,] and fell down the stairs.

When we have read all the books, when we have considered all the arguments, when we have drafted and sifted all the plans, we come to that dreadful moment when there is nothing else to do but begin writing.

(8) In marking off non-restrictive (non-defining) relative clauses:

People such as barmen, who work late into the night, are seldom early risers.

The writers of Greece and Rome, from whom we have inherited many of our ideas about literature, believed composition to be an art with rules.

These examples could be zero-punctuated, in which case the *who –* and *from whom –* clauses would become restrictive, i.e. would specify 'barmen who work late into the night' and 'writers from whom we have inherited many of our ideas'!

(9) In marking off parenthetical clauses:

The college buildings, if a row of derelict sheds could be called by that name, lay in a hollow.

This illustrates the use of the comma as a suspensive device; the topic is further explored in Section 4 below.

(10) In marking off verbless clauses used adjectivally:

Their hostess, radiant as ever, was waiting to greet them.

Eager for a bargain, the tourist reached for his wallet.

She turned away, furious.

(11) In marking off adverbial clauses:

> When I had read the book [,] I decided to visit some of the places described in it.

> Although Latin is no longer a compulsory subject [,] every student of our language should try to learn a little.

It is generally possible to omit the comma when the dependent clause comes first. When it follows the main clause problems of antecedence may arise. These are not always solved by the simple insertion of a comma:

> I decided to visit some of the places described in the book [,] as soon as I had read it.

Omission of the comma would strongly suggest that *visit* is the antecedent of *as soon as*, etc. The comma would not of itself firmly establish the antecedence of *decided*. That could be more convincingly done by placing the *as soon as* construction immediately after *decided*, with the option of commas (to suggest a parenthetical addition) or zero (clearly suggesting the bond of verb and adverbial):

> I decided [,] as soon as I had read it [,] to visit some of the places described in the book.

(12) In marking off participle clauses:

> Summoning all his strength [,] he rose from the chair.

> While driving to Scotland [,] she met with an accident.

When a clause with the present participle leads the sentence, the comma may be omitted; indeed, participle clauses expressing time or duration (e.g. the second example above) are usually so punctuated, the comma being reserved for expressive purposes. A temporal clause in the end-position is not usually marked off by a comma:

> She met with an accident while driving to Scotland.

> She broke off the engagement after meeting her prospective father-in-law.

Clauses with the past participle generally require the comma:

> Deprived of his pension, he lived in wretched dependence on charitable bodies.

Mozart died in obscurity, forgotten by the fashionable world.

Zero punctuation may be possible when the past participle clause expresses a condition or possibility:

Given the chance I should love to visit China. (= 'If I were given the chance')

Deprived of his books he would die of boredom. (= 'If he were deprived of his books', 'Without his books')

(13) Optionally, to mark off infinitive clauses:

To secure the boat [,] he put out a stern-line.

To find the answer [,] turn to the end of the book.

The comma option is more likely in the second instance, where it marks an instruction, than in the first. The balance of choice shifts when the dependent clause is moved to the end of the sentence:

He put out a stern-line [,] to secure the boat.

The comma would perhaps be used only if the action described in the main clause appeared to require some comment or explanation. But at least the comma is a possibility. This is hardly the case with:

Turn to the end of the book to find the answer.

Infinitive clauses commenting on or evaluating a statement are marked off with a comma:

To be strictly honest, I am no grammarian.

Here the clause is a kind of disjunct (cf. the illustrations in 2.13 and 2.15). Infinitive clauses used adverbially are zero-punctuated:

To tell the truth I would need access to private papers.
(= 'In order to tell the truth', 'before I could tell the truth')

Note that when an infinitive clause forms the subject or object of a sentence, it is never disjoined by a comma:

To read Dante is a worthy ambition.

Every morning I try to start the boiler.

As a rule complements are also zero-punctuated, though here practice varies with cases:

To live in the Midlands is to risk pneumonia.

His keenest ambition was [,] to become a successful writer.

In the first of these two examples, the clause *to risk pneumonia* is unambiguously the complement of the subject *To live in the Midlands* – just as *damp* complements *Leicestershire* in *Leicestershire is damp*. Hence the omission of any comma. In the second example there is certainly a complementary relationship between *His keenest ambition* and *to become a successful writer*, but if a comma is used it has the purport of a specifying mark, slightly weaker than a colon or a dash. (Compare *His keenest ambition was: to become a successful writer*, and *His keenest ambition was – to become a successful writer*.) When the relationship between clauses is that of a reporting expression (e.g. *the answer is, the secret is, the idea was*) followed by the thing reported (*to wash regularly, to use talcum powder, to smell nice*) the comma often occurs as a mark of citation. (See section 4 below.)

Note that *is to* and *was to* are particled auxiliaries, related in meaning to *will* and *would*, expressing future time from a present or past standpoint. (*He is to speak at a conference in New Mexico* = 'will speak', 'will be speaking'; *She was to become the outstanding pianist of her day* = 'would become', 'eventually became'). The overlap of this particled verb-form with the to-infinitive can give rise to ambiguities that must be resolved with the help of a comma:

The idea is to save millions of pounds.
(= 'The idea will save millions')

The idea is, to save millions of pounds.
(= 'This is the idea')

(14) Optionally, in marking off noun clauses occurring as 'fronted' direct objects (see 2.5):

What thoughts went through my mind [,] I leave you to imagine.

> How the poor are to survive [,] no one will say.
>
> Where the money will come from [,] only God and the Chancellor know.

In their 'unmarked' position, these constructions would not take the comma:

> I leave you to imagine what thoughts went through my mind.
>
> No one will say how the poor are to survive.
>
> Only God and the Chancellor know where the money will come from.

Clauses functioning as sentence subjects are never disjoined by a comma from the ensuing verb:

> What you say about Byron interests me.
>
> How the poor will survive is a question no one cares to answer.
>
> Where the money will come from does not concern us.

(v) *Zero*

What we here call 'zero' is no mere neglect of punctuation; it is a positive option, usually taken as an alternative to the comma, and has distinct syntactic and expressive values. The ordinary writer is bound to be as conservative and circumspect about this as he would be about any other mark of punctuation. Literary talent can afford to take brilliant liberties:

> That afternoon there was a party of tourists at the Terrace and looking down in the water among the empty beer-cans and dead barracudas a woman saw a great long white spine with a huge tail at the end that lifted and swung with the tide while the east wind blew a heavy steady sea outside the entrance to the harbour.

This is a single paragraph, consisting of a single sentence, consisting of an unbroken thread of constructions, from Hemingway's *The Old Man and the Sea*. There are no commas where conservative practice might indicate their use, no nervous concessions to lurking options, e.g.:

> That afternoon there was a party of tourists at the Terrace, and looking down in the water [,] among the empty beer-cans and dead barracudas [,] a woman saw a great long white spine with a huge tail at the end that lifted and swung with the tide [,] while the east wind blew a heavy, steady sea outside the entrance to the harbour.

There is in Hemingway's design a logic which is immediately apparent from the long sequence *a great long white spine with a huge tail at the end that lifted and swung with the tide.* Here successive constructions are dependently bound to a preceding expression: *a great long white spine*; *a spine with a huge tail at the end*; *a tail that lifted and swung with the tide.* Zero punctuation denotes the chain of dependence. Similarly, there is no expressive comma after *tide*, because the adverbial clause (*while the east wind blew*, etc.) is tightly bound to its antecedents, *lifted* and *swung* (the sense being *lifted and swung while the east wind blew*, with *while* as temporal adverb, not as a mere coordinating conjunction).

One common consequence of omitting marks of punctuation is to invite ambivalent readings. This is also true of the Hemingway passage, where, however, the writing is not marred but made richer by the possibility of multiple interpretations:

> . . . looking down in the water among the empty beer-cans and dead barracudas a woman saw a great long white spine with a huge tail at the end . . .

The zero punctuation allows a dual perspective: on the woman *looking down . . . among the empty beer cans*, etc., and on the long spine *lying . . . among the empty beer-cans*, etc. Further, the woman looks down at, and the spine lies in, *the water among the empty beer-cans.* There is a sleight of hand in the unstopped writing.

### 4 Suspensions

Stops mark junctures, indicate continuities, clarify relationships. The mark of suspension is a kind of compound stop, isolating an expression that momentarily intrudes on the straightforward progress of the text – a parenthesis, an apposition, some qualifying phrase, some explanation or afterthought. The marks principally used for this purpose are the comma, the dash, and the bracket. They offer the writer a small, graded set of expressive choices:

> His colleagues, for whom he always expressed the greatest respect, ignored his work.
>
> His colleagues – for whom he always expressed the greatest respect – ignored his work.
>
> His colleagues (for whom he always expressed the greatest respect) ignored his work.

These versions may be interpreted as different 'scorings' (see section 5 below) of an imagined vocal delivery, with variations of tempo, intonation, and voice quality. There are varying levels in the depth, so to speak, of the parenthesis.

A less common way of scoring an interruptive construction is by using the triple dot:

> I thought of my daughter . . . for so long a stranger to me . . . and I felt sad.

The dots are highly expressive, suggesting quite a pronounced pause and giving the parenthesis a reflective, even distracted character. The triple dot is also an artful, quasi-dramatic mark of *citation*:

> She opened the cupboard and revealed . . . a large bone.

The example shows the suspensive value of the marking; the dots suggest the imminence of a revelation for which the reader must consent to wait. In addition to saying 'wait', however, the dots also say 'namely'. Like the colon in one of its commonest uses, they cite a case or an example. In that use the colon may be rivalled by the dash and the comma:

> There are two precious things in a man's life: his family and his work.
>
> There are two precious things in a man's life – his family and his work.

> There are two precious things in a man's life, his family and his work.

The act of citation is conveyed most strongly by the first example; the third version is the weakest, and as a rule this 'light' punctuation with a comma should be avoided because of the danger of ambiguous or slurred meaning:

> Two elements are necessary in life, work and play.

Here a colon or a dash would clearly be preferable to the comma.

## 5 Scorings

There remain a few marks of punctuation which are used wholly or principally to 'score' the text, projecting intonation, accentuation, tempo, and the general style of delivery. The comma, dash, and bracket have their value as scoring devices, as well as discharging other punctuational tasks. Further scorings are provided by marks of exclamation and interrogation, by the triple dot, and by inverted commas, underlinings, or changes of type-face:

> She felt – what was the word? – 'depleted'.
> It was a 'good' book (and he *hated* 'good' books!).

The exclamation point, question mark, and inverted comma are sometimes to be read as placatory gestures, querying a turn of phrase, apologizing for some oddity, owning up to a not wholly appropriate or perhaps excessively colloquial expression:

> The woman identified herself as the 'proprietrix' (!) of the café.

> The doves (?) of our present economic regime are the Conservative 'wets'.

Cursory examination of the correspondence columns of our daily newspaper suggests a current tendency to use inverted commas over-zealously, as though apologizing for perfectly acceptable usages. They are of course appropriate marks of direct quotation from literary works:

The 'lowing herd' moved about us in the twilight.

But there is no need to use them in shamefaced acknowledgment of the unliterary facts of life:

In the 'shippon' we could hear the cows 'mooing'.

It is very difficult to score a text effectively, and as a rule writers are well advised to be conservative in the use of these marks. Among twentieth-century authors, one of the most brilliant exponents of bold scoring is Virginia Woolf. The following passage from *Mrs Dalloway* illustrates her skill in projecting the voice behind the words:

> What Sally felt was simply this. She had owed Clarissa an enormous amount. They had been friends, not acquaintances, friends, and she still saw Clarissa all in white going about the house with her hands full of flowers – to this day tobacco plants made her think of Bourton. But – did Peter understand? – she lacked something. Lacked what was it? She had charm; she had extraordinary charm. But to be frank (and she felt that Peter was an old friend, a real friend – did absence matter? did distance matter? She had often wanted to write to him, but torn it up, yet felt he understood, for people understand without things being said, as one realizes growing old, and old she was, had been that afternoon to see her sons at Eton, where they had the mumps), to be quite frank, then, how could Clarissa have done it? – married Richard Dalloway? a sportsman, a man who cared only for dogs. Literally, when he came into the room he smelt of the stables. And then all this? She waved her hand.

Here the comma and the semi-colon are scoring marks; points of exclamation and interrogation make their signs of speech-melody; the dash is used to break off comment with after-comment. The boldest treatment in the whole passage, however, is reserved for the bracket. A long parenthesis begins in the middle of a sentence, after the words *to be frank*, and closes towards the end of the next sentence, before the phrase *to be quite frank, then*, which marks the resumption of a thread of discourse. Virginia Woolf's scoring in this extraordinary instance is not the conventional indication of lowered pitch or throwaway delivery; its a mark of characterization, of tactics in a social interaction. It suggests a divided purpose in the speaker, Sally, who wishes to criticize her old friend Clarissa, but needs to secure a base of confidence by making herself agreeable to her old friend Peter. Punctuation here outruns common usage and expresses the psychology of a character.

Indeed, this chapter begins and ends with examples that take us beyond 'common usage' and into the realms of literary art. But everyday practice is what must concern us; the sensitivity and skill of a Waugh or a Woolf are granted to few. The common practitioner labours by rule, and struggles to come to terms with the shifting intricacies of language. Sometimes he follows a blundering instinct. Sometimes he seeks authority. And it is when he enjoys the security of authoritarian assurance that he becomes, alas, most vulnerable.

# 6
# Authorities: Under which king?

Under which king, Bezonian? speak, or die!
                – Pistol, in *King Henry IV, Part II*

Say this. Shut up. O'Grady says this,
You talk fast without thinking what to say.
What goes is what I say O'Grady says.

Or let me rather put the point like this:
O'Grady says what goes is what I say
O'Grady says; that's what O'Grady says.
              – Kingsley Amis, 'The Voice of Authority'

### 1 The ghost of O'Grady

We have a tradition, going back to the eighteenth century, of commentary on 'good' usage and 'correct' style – or rather, on the allegedly bad and incorrect; for what is good is often taken as self-evident. During the past eighty years, the tradition has been elaborated in various handbooks, one of the most influential of which – the godfather of the family, so to speak – has been H.W. and F.G. Fowler's *The King's English*, first published in 1906 and since then periodically reissued, most recently in 1979. The importance of such handbooks is not to be denied; some, like Sir Ernest Gowers' writings on *Plain Words*, well deserve their popularity. All writings on usage, however, breed a spirit that is at once submissive and authoritarian. They are eagerly studied by many who crave the sanction of an authority, and they tend to satisfy that craving. The authors of manuals are forever haunted by the ghost of O'Grady; try as we will to break free, we are obliged to insist on saying what we think he says. We may not be authorities, but we do tend to become authoritarians. Without wishing to presume, we lay down the law, and the experience is dangerously enjoyable.

One of O'Grady's messages is that there is a standard literary idiom, which is the arbiter of usage. The notion is as vague as its parent concept of Standard English, but handbooks on usage imply it repeatedly. Gowers refers to 'a reasonably good standard of writing', and insists that 'such a standard can be attained by anyone with a little effort' (*CPW*, 22). Eric Partridge writes of a 'Literary Standard' which is 'the more conventional, stylized, and dignified, more accurate and logical, sometimes the more beautiful form that Received Standard assumes'. He defines 'Received Standard' as the kind of English that 'fulfils all the requirements of good speech' (*UA*, 306). He does concede, however, that spoken English and spoken American are 'too often criticized as though it were impossible for them to have any laws of their own – a freedom not shackled at every turn by the rules explicit or implicit in Literary Standard' (*UA*, 306). The American E.B. White sturdily comments: 'Writing good standard English is no cinch, and before you have managed it you will have encountered enough rough country to satisfy even the most adventurous spirit' (*ES*, 84). White, an able and witty man – Thurber's colleague on the staff of the *New Yorker* – was presumably teasing the freshman with his *no cinch* (*cinch* being hardly a 'standard English' item); but how could he ignore the phonetic clash of *enough rough*, and why, by his own standards of economy ('avoid the use of qualifiers', he rules) is *the most* pointlessly qualified by *even*? This is what happens to O'Gradymen. Time and again, we rulers feel the pinch of our own regulations. Our only way out is O'Grady's master-saying: 'Don't do as I do, do as I say.'

## 2 From prescription through perplexity to paralysis

A few *do's* and *don'ts* may go a long way; and possibly rules of style and usage are like the doctor's placebos, empty dosages that nevertheless give the patient confidence to surmount his troubles. A general regime of prescriptiveness, on the other hand, will reduce the sufferer to a state of sore perplexity. It breeds two evils. It instils, for one thing, a notion that there is an 'educated class' of 'intelligent speakers' and 'good writers', who determine the wisdoms of usage and style. This idea is rarely put into so many words. Nevertheless, it is difficult to read the manuals without sometimes having the uncomfortable feeling that 'good speaking' and 'good writing' have been assimilated to the other codes of conduct that typify and fortify a class – the middle class. There is a tacit claim to exclusive rights in the language, and hence to a form of social ascendancy. The less affluent or well-schooled – those called by the Fowlers 'the vast number of people who are incapable of appreciating fine shades of meaning' (*KE*, 58) – are intimidated by the discourse of teachers, doctors, lawyers, clergymen, civil servants, council officials, smooth commercial faces and old political hands. They feel that they are verbally impoverished and that they express themselves badly; and they go on believing this while every day they demonstrate their skill in narrative, their talent for repartee, their vivid imagery, their gift for the exact and annihilating phrase. An attentive stroll through a street market is a pleasure the Fowlers might have afforded themselves, before venturing to speak of fine shades of meaning.

The second evil afflicts the would-be writer. Prescription addresses itself to the particulars of writing, and seldom considers the whole pattern. It ignores the structure of composition, in which choices are adapted to contexts, a weakness is offset by a compensatory strength, and a local difficulty yields to a discursive solution. It insists on the occasional *do* and the everlasting damnable *don't* of the isolated detail. It insidiously transforms recommendations into prohibitions. It makes a problem out of writing a phrase, a hazard out of constructing a sentence, a vexation out of building a paragraph. It knocks the joy out of writing, and cripples the active skill. It spooks the writer with such fear of error that he can hardly begin to put words onto paper. No one should expect writing to be easy, but it is immeasurably important to have some initial fluency in composition; to be able to construct first and refine afterwards. There is no fluency when the making of every sentence is attended by worried questions – 'Is this a cliché?' 'Ought I to find another word?' 'Ought I to write *ought I*, or should it be *should*?' There are baffled pauses, of increasing length, culminating in paralysis.

### 3 Negative prescriptions

One of the most discouraging practices of the authoritarian is and negative prescription – and nearly all prescriptions are negatively framed. (The third chapter of this book provides examples.) There is a bony finger in *don't*, and something worse, a discreetly patronizing murmur, in *avoid*. Things that should *not* be done, or should be *avoided* wherever possible, become more important than things that *might* be done; though the rule-givers will insist that they are clarifying *can* by expounding *cannot*. Thus the Fowlers, after a long discussion of so-called 'malaprops':

> We have touched shortly upon four dozen of what we call malaprops. Now possible malaprops, in our extended sense, are to be reckoned not by the dozen but by the million. Moreover, out of our four dozen, not more than some half a dozen are uses that it is worth any one's while to register individually in his mind for avoidance. The conclusion of which is this: we have made no attempt at cataloguing mistakes of this sort that must not be committed; every one must construct his own catalogue by care, observation, and the resolve to use no word whose meaning he is not sure of – even though that resolve bring on him the extreme humiliation of now and then opening the dictionary. Our aim has been, not to make a list, but to inculcate a frame of mind. (*KE*, 28)

This is archly written and speciously argued; a fair example of having your cake and demurely eating it. In places the style slips into nonsense by negation: 'we have made no attempt at cataloguing mistakes of this sort that must not be committed'. (Are there then mistakes that *may* be committed? And what is meant by 'no attempt at cataloguing'? After a censorious review of four dozen instances, under seven headings, occupying ten pages of print? *Garn*, as the vast number of the unrefined would say.) The argument turns on the need to be positively negative, a philosophy expressed in this extraordinary sentence:

Moreover, out of our four dozen, not more than some half a dozen are uses that it is worth any one's while to register individually in his mind for avoidance.

The master phrase is 'register individually in his mind for avoidance'. It tells us that we are to learn by systematically noting what not to learn. The joy of not doing, the delight of refusing a good chance to make a false move, is frequently expressed in *The King's English*. Chapter II begins with an almost regretful statement about case in nouns: 'There is not much opportunity for going wrong here, because we have shed most of our cases' (*KE*,69). The *opportunity for going wrong* is the essence of O'Grady's game.

### 4 Myths

O'Grady is also an expert in the prescriptive myth. There is, for example, a somewhat tangled mythology of *however* and its preferred position in the sentence. Partridge states:

> HOWEVER comes, not at the end of a sentence or clause ('He refuse further refreshment, however', Inez Irwin, *The Poison Cross Mystery*, 1936), but after the first significant unit, as in 'He, however, did not think so' (emphasis on 'He'), 'He flinched, however, when the gun went off' (although he had shown himself calm up to that point) . . . (*UA*, 144–5)

He outlaws the end-position, but says nothing about the possibility of putting *however* at the beginning of the sentence. On this, Strunk and White give a firm ruling:

> HOWEVER. Avoid starting a sentence with *however* when the meaning is 'nevertheless'. The word usually serves better when not in the first position. (*ES*,48)

How the word 'serves better' when not in the first position is not immediately clear. However, the authors give examples. First a faulty specimen:

> The roads were almost impassable. However, we at last succeeded in reaching camp.

Then the corrected text, in which the word allegedly 'serves better':

> The roads were almost impassable. At last, however, we succeeded in reaching camp. (*ES*,49)

They add:

> When *however* comes first, it means 'in whatever way' or 'to whatever extent'

and cite:

> However you advise him, he will probably do as he thinks best.
>
> However discouraging the prospect, he never lost heart.

But this is fudging grammar to win a point. In *however you advise him*, *however* is an adverb of manner, and in *however discouraging* it is an intensifier. Neither of these functions is relevant to its use as a conjunct (when the meaning is 'nevertheless').

Partridge frowns on the practice of ending a sentence with conjunct *however*; Strunk and White object to beginning a sentence with it; and English writers go on breaking these rules, the origin of which may be sought in the praxis of classical Latin. In Latin prose, *autem* ('however') always follows 'the first significant element' in the sentence. Classical models influenced English prose and English precept in the eighteenth and nineteenth centuries; and that, presumably, is how the myth of *however* has grown. There is no reason why it should only be permitted to accentuate 'the first significant element' of an English clause. It can be used to focus different pieces of text, and hence to imply various meanings:

> Bill and Ron missed the meeting. However, they will be there tomorrow.

(The contrasting emphasis of *however* takes the whole of the preceding sentence into scope. It suggests the meaning 'Despite that . . . ', or, colloquially, 'Never mind'; 'Don't worry, though . . . ')

> Bill and Ron missed the meeting. Ron, however, will be there tomorrow.

(This is Partridge's accentuation of the 'first significant element'. The implication is 'Ron, but not Bill'.)

> Bill and Ron missed the meeting. One of them will be there tomorrow, however.

(The focus is on *tomorrow*; and the placing of the conjunct directs the focus.)

This is not what O'Grady says. These are common intuitions about the semantics of English.

Another piece of myth-making concerns the allegedly improper use of *while* as a contrastive or concessive conjunction, roughly equivalent to *whereas* and *although*: e.g. *Jill chose a false moustache, while Mary preferred something less provocative* (= 'whereas'); *While I love animals, I do wish Henry wouldn't let his iguana lie on the bed* (= 'although'). Partridge damns the 'although' sense:

> WHILE for *although* is a perverted use of the correct sense of *while*, which properly means 'at the same time as', during the same time that'. (*UA*,369)

'Perverted' is a heavy boot, and 'properly' is a good prescriptivist bludgeon. Strunk and White propound a comparable doctrine:

> WHILE. Avoid the indiscriminate use of the word for *and*, *but*, and *although*. Many writers use it frequently as a substitute for *and* and *but*, either from a mere desire to vary the connective, or from doubt about which of the two connectives is the more appropriate. In this use it is best replaced by a semi-colon. (*ES*,63)

'Indiscriminate' is at least kinder than 'perverted', and it is useful to suggest the option of a semi-colon. They give an example of 'indiscriminate' *while*:

> The office and salesrooms are on the ground floor, while the rest of the building is used for manufacturing

And suggest as a better version:

> The office and salesrooms are on the ground floor; the rest of the building is used for manufacturing.

They look quite tolerantly on the use of *while* in the meaning 'although', stating their principle thus:

> Its use as a virtual equivalent of *although* is allowable in sentences where this leads to no ambiguity or absurdity. (*ES*,63)

They illustrate:

> While I admire his energy, I wish it were employed in a better cause.

So far, so good; but their comment on this example is an ingenious piece of special pleading, based on the begged question of what *while* 'properly' means. They say 'This is entirely correct as is shown by the paraphrase', and their paraphrase reads:

> I admire his energy; at the same time I wish it were employed in a better cause.

But the paraphrase only 'shows' by assuming the point it sets out to show. This is the shaky premise for a further ramshackle demonstration. The authors cite, as incorrect:

> While the temperature reaches 90 or 95 degrees in the daytime, the nights are often chilly.

Repeating their earlier argument, they declare that 'The paraphrase shows why the use of *while* is incorrect', and they demonstrate:

> The temperature reaches 90 or 95 degrees in the daytime; at the same time the nights are often chilly.

But again, the paraphrase obediently 'shows' what we are asked to assume for the purpose of making the paraphrase, i.e. that *while* 'properly' means 'at the same time that', or 'during the time that'. This 'proper' meaning is an O'Grady phantom. Does anyone really believe that the sentence *Some like jelly while others like jam* 'properly means' that these predilections are manifested simultaneously? The common user of the common tongue has more sense than his mentors. He may not have the grammatical terms at his finger-tips, but he knows how to operate *while* as a temporal conjunction, and how to use it as a contrastive, and he is not confused. He has wit enough to see that a sentence like *Jack Sprat ate fat meat while his wife ate lean* is possibly ambiguous, and he perceives that *while* is a common journalistic substitute for *and* (*Mrs Hawkins was responsible for the flower arrangements, while refreshments were provided by the Young Wives' Club*); but no one will bully or bamboozle him into supposing that the weather is hot during the time when it is cold.

The ruling on *while* is one of those doctrines that pass from textbook to textbook, in some cases circumventing the ascertainable facts of usage. H.W. Fowler's monumental work *A Dictionary of Modern English Usage* (first published in 1926) contains a long entry on *while*, including this statement:

> . . . the temporal sense that lurks in *while* may lead those who use it into the absurdity of seeming to say that two events occurred, or will occur simultaneously which cannot possibly do so. *The early morning will be rather cold while afternoon temperatures will rise to the seasonal average.* (*MEU*,707)

Strunk and White's argument is here anticipated, with an illustration remarkably like theirs. And if we consult *The King's English*, we find the Fowlers warning against 'the indiscriminate use of while' (*KE*,199); Strunk and White, in a noticeably similar phrase, warn students to avoid 'the indiscriminate use of this word' (*EU*,63). These small examples point to the great power of books to prolong the life of shadowy notions. Judgments, examples, even wordings, are passed on from text to text, and in time the strength of this inter-textual tradition seems to overpower the force of common observation. Instead of trying to establish what speakers actually say, we go to X to discover what X says they say; and our confidence in X is all the greater when it appears that X says what X thinks Y says about what speakers say, or ought to say. This is the triumph of O'Grady.

### 5 Who's the insider?

O'Grady says who's in and who's out; and this is the unacceptable face of O'Grady. It is difficult for anyone to write about usage without betraying some prejudice – against journalists, perhaps, or educationists, or sociologists, or any other kind of 'ist', but in general against 'the others', who belong to a different class, went to a different kind of school, have different opinions, different aspirations, different attitudes to the past, different interpretations of the present. 'The others', with their irritating claims to a fair hearing, lurk behind many an assertion:

> ENTHUSE is to be avoided, though it has its apologists. (*UA*,107)

Partridge's tone is dismissive. Who are these apologists? And why not call them 'advocates'? Had he written ENTHUSE *is to be avoided, though some people defend the usage*, the statement might not have aroused the feeling that an outsider is having the door shut in his face. *Apologist* conveys something more than 'one who defends by argument'; through association with *apology* it has acquired the sense of 'one who makes excuses', or even 'one who argues on behalf of the strictly indefensible'. The apologists to whom Partridge refers are 'the others', the incorrigibly mistaken.

The fault of 'the others' is that they are not *ordinary* or *average*. Those words are dear to O'Gradymen, On the subject of *woolliness*, Partridge writes

> The ideal at which a writer should aim – admittedly it is impossible of attainment – is that he write so clearly, so precisely, so unambiguously, that his words can bear only one meaning to all averagely intelligent readers that possess an average knowledge of the language used. (*UA*,372)

It would have been enough (and less woolly) to have said that 'a writer must try to say exactly what he means'; but all those 'averagely intelligent readers' with their 'average knowledge' (not a swot or a troublesome egghead among them) have to be brought into the discussion. They signify the insiders, 'people like you and me'. Partridge continues:

> But to generalize further on woolliness would serve no useful purpose. I shall particularize by giving, first a number of brief examples, and, in most cases, commenting on them, and, secondly, some longer passages and leaving them to the reader's angry bewilderment. (*UA*,372)

The averagely intelligent reader is now conspiratorially invited to be bewildered, and, being bewildered, to feel angry. But the passages Partridge goes on to cite are not bewildering (the average reader can understand them with an average application of his average knowledge), and do not incite anger. They are verbose, and sometimes illogical, and it is interesting to attempt revisions. 'Angry bewilderment', however, forestalls the benevolent neutrality of 'interesting', and dictates a hostile stance.

The stance is that of the decently educated representative of the middle class. In *The King's English*, the Fowlers make the following observation about slang:

> To the ordinary man, of average intelligence and middle-class position, slang comes from every direction, from above, from below, and from all sides, as well as from the centre. (*KE*,58)

So: slang comes from above (royalty? the peerage? the episcopacy?); from below (the workers, the masses); from all sides (the professions, commerce, the universities, the better sort of newspaper); and even from the *centre* (i.e. not from the ordinary man's digestive tract, but from the deepest ranks of the middle class). Here is a Ptolemaic view of the linguistic universe, putting the averagely intelligent middle-class citizen at the hub of it all. Like Partridge, the Fowlers make conspiratorial overtures to their readers. For instance, after reviewing some examples of the 'compound prepositional style' (involving the use of expressions like *in view of, with regard to, for the purpose of*), they comment:

> Of these the first is correct; but the sentence it comes in is so typical of the compound-prepositional style that no one who reads it will be surprised that its patrons should sometimes get mixed; how should people who write like that keep their ideas clear? (*KE*,177)

'Patrons' patronizes; the cinema, the bingo hall, and the pub have patrons. 'People who write like that' represent, like Partridge's 'apologists', 'the others'. (*No one who reads it* implies the consent of that obliging spirit, the averagely intelligent reader.) The outsiders cannot win. A usage is acknowledged to be 'correct', but at the same time is said to be 'typical' of 'people who cannot keep their ideas clear'. In this passage, the Fowlers themselves are not masterly expositors of the clear idea. *Patrons . . . sometimes get mixed* is both inelegant and ambiguous. But O'Grady will always catch O'Grady, and that matters little; it is a hazard of the game. What is much less acceptable is an implied division of the speaking population into 'people like us' and 'persons of that sort'.

### 6 Polonian precepts

O'Grady has a scheme to encourage the deserving; he proposes to the student a few simple recommendations to see him through his perplexities. 'Stick to these and you won't go far wrong' is the message; or, as Polonius puts it, in another connection,

And these few precepts in thy memory
See thou character.

The Fowlers set the example, with a list of 'practical rules in the domain of vocabulary'. The rules are:

Prefer the familiar word to the far-fetched.
Prefer the concrete word to the abstract.
Prefer the single word to the circumlocution.
Prefer the short word to the long.
Prefer the Saxon word to the Romance. (*KE*,11)

The list has been much discussed, and has found its way, in various forms, into many later writings on usage. Sir Arthur Quiller-Couch refers to the Fowlerian rules in his lectures *On the Art of Writing* (*AW*,137). George Orwell, in his essay on 'Politics and the English Language,' propounds a comparable list:

i. Never use a metaphor, simile, or other figure of speech which you are used to seeing in print.
ii. Never use a long word when a short one will do.
iii. If it is possible to cut a word out, always cut it out.
iv. Never use the passive when you can use the active.
v. Never use a foreign phrase, a scientific word, or a

jargon word if you can think of an everyday English equivalent.
vi. Break any of these rules sooner than say anything outright barbarous. (*CE*,4, 139)

*Prefer* has turned to *never*; and the last rule is what is known in current slang as a *cop-out*; but the influence of the Fowlers is obvious. Strunk and White echo the rules in their 'elementary principles of composition', where they recommend students to –

Use the active voice.
Put statements in positive form.
Use definite, specific, concrete language.
Omit needless words. (*ES*,18–25)

Sir Ernest Gowers presents three rules, expressing, as he puts it, 'the essence of the matter' in questions of vocabulary. Again, we have glimpses of *The King's English*, in precept and wording:

Use no more words than are necessary to express your meaning, for if you use more you are likely to obscure it and to tire your reader. In particular do not use superfluous adjectives and adverbs and do not use roundabout phrases where single words would serve.

Use familiar words rather than the far-fetched, if they express your meaning equally well; for the familiar are more likely to be readily understood.

Use words with a precise meaning rather than those that are vague, for they will obviously serve better to make your meaning clear; and in particular prefer concrete words to abstract, for they are more likely to have a precise meaning. (*CPW*,80)

There is obviously a general agreement, among these commentators, about basic principles of composition. Now no one would deny that such a list of recommendations can be very helpful, whether as a support in moments of doubt, or as a programme for self-criticism. Having made his rules, however, O'Grady has a human tendency to renege, or qualify. Orwell, as noted above, advises his readers to break any of his rules 'sooner than say anything outright barbarous'.

(*Barbarous* thereby joins the ranks of disapproving words like *woolly*, *muddy*, and *turgid*). The Fowlers write:

> The fact remains . . . that different kinds of composition require different treatment; but any attempt to go into details on the question would be too ambitious; the reader can only be warned that in this fact may be found good reasons for sometimes disregarding any or all of the preceding rules. Moreover, they must not be applied either so unintelligently as to sacrifice any really important shade of meaning, or so invariably as to leave an impression of monotonous and unrelieved emphasis. (KE,17)

Here again, a saving clause ('they must not be applied . . . so unintelligently as to sacrifice any really important shade of meaning') forestalls criticism, What the Fowlers had in mind, presumably, was something every O'Grady must concede: that all the precepts in the world will not add up to a practice. Or as O'Grady says on p.55 of this book, 'a style cannot be taught by rule or made by recipe.'

## 7 Received wisdoms, reduced perceptions

Polonius has his wisdom, and wisdom should always be respected. When, however, wise recommendations are circulated without commentary, elaboration, or qualification, they become received wisdoms, in the spirit of 'do this because this is the right thing to do'. Received wisdoms are often expressed in drastic forms – e.g. Strunk and White's bald injunction to 'Use the active voice' – and these strict maxims tend to reduce our perceptions of language and its manifold resources. The Fowlers tell their readers to 'prefer the familiar word to the far fetched'. Sir Ernest Gowers repeats this prescription, but adds a saving commentary, 'if they express your meaning equally well; for the familiar are more likely to be readily understood.' Gowers' explanation provides at least a little support for his rule. The Fowlers' bare command leaves much at issue, including the fact that what is far-fetched to one is quite familiar to another. The student may be encouraged to condemn as 'far-fetched' any word he has not previously come across, and to reject as turgid or boring all writing couched in unfamiliar terms. The huge vocabulary of English is at his disposal, and he is apparently urged to ignore most of it. The received wisdom leads to a reduced perception (also fostered by the rule 'Prefer the short word to the long'), which might be expressed in the form 'Big words are bunk' or 'If I don't know it, it must be unnecessary.'

Two of the recurrent wisdoms invite particular commentary, for they subsume the others. One is the recommendation to 'prefer concrete words to the abstract'; the other, the instruction 'never use the passive when you can use the active. Proscriptions of 'far-fetched words,' 'long words', 'jargon words', 'foreign words', 'Romance words' (i.e. those of Latin or Greek origin) are in essence warnings against abstraction. Cautionary remarks on 'circumlocutions', 'roundabout phrases', 'needless words', etc., reflect the fact that certain types of construction, of which the passive is an obvious representative, seem wordy. (In fact the passive is no more 'roundabout', by wordcount, than some other constructions of the verb phrase.)

(a) *Abstract words*

The case against abstract words is properly a case against dishonesty and pretentiousness. George Orwell was right to deplore the evasiveness of a usage that can explain away the bombing of a village, and the killing of innocent people, as *pacification*. We should look coldly on all institutional or professional attempts to hide the inconvenient fact in muffling abstractions. We should question, for example, the doctors' bland manipulation of meaning when they describe as *adjuvant therapy* the use of drugs to attack conditions that have not been cured by major surgery. The very use of *condition* to mean 'serious or chronic illness' is a kind of emollient abstraction, as is *the management of the condition*, which means 'keeping the patient going'. (Except in the phrase *management of a terminal condition*, which means 'helping the patient to go'.)

Abstractions are rightly condemned when they are a means of lying, deception, and professional euphemism. They are also fairly criticized as the common resort of pretentiousness. If I declare that *The mobilization of existent facilities and resources is mandatory under current circumstances*, meaning

'We must make do with what we have', I have only myself to blame when some people cannot understand a word I say, others laugh at me, and one or two would like to hit me. This is the affection called *abstractitis* in *A Dictionary of Modern English Usage*. The examples given under that heading, and others listed in the article called *sociologese*, defy any attempt at a defence.

The Polonian warning against abstractions is admirable, so far. But is it really the case that abstract words are bad?; is it not rather that some people use them in a bad way – the way we commonly stigmatize as *jargon*? Ah, says O'Grady, but bad users are nurtured by bad habits of use; language works retroactively on the mind. This is how Quiller-Couch puts it:

> A lesson about writing your language may go deeper than language; for language . . . is your reason, your λόγοϐ. So long as you prefer abstract words, which express other men's summarized concepts of things, to concrete ones which lie as near as can be reached to things themselves and are the first-hand material for your thoughts, you will remain, at the best, writers at second-hand. If your language be jargon your intellect, if not your whole character, will almost certainly correspond. (*AW,103*)

This implies a naive theory of language, presents a dubious view of the relationship between language and thought, and, with a slick homiletic turn, makes language the moral determinant of character. It was written long before courses in Linguistics were part of any university curriculum. Its arguments now wear a discredited look, and yet the theology of the wicked abstraction persists to this day. The tenets are:

(i) Concrete words are more precise than abstract words (or as Gowers puts it, 'are more likely to have a precise meaning').
(ii) Imprecise words permit vague thoughts.
(iii) Vague thinking is bad for the character.
(iv) Therefore abstract words are bad for the character and will make you devious, inert, and unnaturally addicted to nouns. Quiller-Couch says 'where your mind should go straight, it will dodge' (*AW*,103). Gowers cites G.M. Young to the effect that 'an excessive reliance on

the noun . . . will, in the end, detach the mind from the realities of here and now . . . and insensibly induce the habit of abstraction, generalization, and vagueness,' (*CPW*,133). Marijuana and glue-sniffing could scarcely have worse effects.

Against these articles an unbeliever can only protest –

i) That abstract words are necessary, and in great numbers, though the power of abstraction is sometimes abused by the pretentious and the dishonest.
(ii) That both abstract and concrete words may be precisely or imprecisely used. There is no proof that concrete words are inherently 'more precise' than abstract words, or that they more effectively mediate experience at 'first hand'. That could only begin to be true if each word we call 'concrete' bore such exclusive reference to a concrete 'thing' as to be integral with it. We know that this is not so; we also know that 'concrete' words are, in varying degrees, abstractions. Even Gowers concedes that 'many concrete words have a penumbra of uncertainty about them' (*CPW*,133).

As to the first point, our language and discourse teem with abstract words which are indispensable. The vocabulary of the emotions and perceptions, of reasoning and cognition, of measurement and calculation, of morality and obligation, is abstract; *love, thought, size, duty,* are all abstractions. We need a host of abstract words to enable us to talk about the intangible things in our experience. We also need them so that we may usefully generalize, including countless particulars in one representation. The effective summary is no less 'precise' than the particular denotation. No one would seriously allege that the saying *Necessity is the mother of invention* is imprecise because of the abstractions *necessity* and *invention*; or that we would somehow come nearer to the first-hand feel of things if we were to translate the proverb into the form *When you're in a fix you soon find a way out*. (Though *fix* is the vaguest of abstractions, and *way* has its penumbra of uncertainty.) The precision of the particular instance is beside the point. It is the value of the generalization to characterize any case of the pressing problem that calls for the ingenious solution.

Quiller-Couch's strictures on the abstract read oddly to anyone browsing through his book. Here is a sample of his habitual style:

> Let me revert to our list of the qualities necessary to good writing, and come to the last – *Persuasiveness*; of which you may say, indeed, that it embraces the whole – not only the qualities of propriety, perspicuity, accuracy, as we have been considering, but many another, such as harmony, order, sublimity, beauty of diction; all in short that – writing being an art, not a science, and therefore so personal a thing – may be summed up under the word *Charm*. (*AW*,35)

*Persuasiveness* is abstract; *charm* is abstract; *quality*, *propriety*, *perspicuity*, *accuracy*, are abstract; there is hardly a noun in this passage that is not abstract. The piece is full of words 'expressing other men's summarized concepts of things' and presumably 'detaching the mind of the writer from the here and now' – but no, these jibes are unfair. The passage simply illustrates the point that we can hardly do without abstract nouns. Certainly Quiller-Couch knew what he meant; his mind was surely not bemused, his thinking not poisoned, by a surfeit of abstractions.

Concrete words can be very vaguely used (*thing* is the obvious instance), and in their vagueness are less precise than many a cloudy abstraction: *He left his things on the beach* could be tantamount to *He left his clothing* or *He left his possessions* or *He left his equipment*. The abstract potential of the concrete word is something to reckon with; it is often hard to decide where concrete ends and abstract begins. If *equipment* is abstract, is *tools* concrete? One might think so, but *tool*, as a superordinate term, is more 'abstract' than *hammer*, *saw*, *plane*, *chisel*, etc.; and to a skilled workman, even *hammer* may be a kind of abstraction, in comparison with the specific *claw hammer*, *ball-peen hammer*, etc. If *concrete* means 'referring to one object', or even 'referring to one type of object', then many of the words we call concrete are relatively abstract. Concrete words, furthermore, are often used to communicate abstractions – for instance, to frame generalizations. We have considered the generalizing power of a proverb using abstract words. Here is a proverb using concrete words: *It's the early bird that catches the worm.* This could only have a concrete, specific meaning if it were used to describe an actual bird in process of catching a factual worm at some early hour of the real clock. It can be safely said that the proverb never has that literal meaning. It is a generalization, used, like all generalizations, to denote a category of events or characteristics.

Concrete words can be vague; concrete words can be used to convey general notions; concrete words can be deceptive; but the conventional warning is always against the abstract The abstract word, it seems, is often blamed for vices that have relatively little to do with its properties of abstraction. If you make war on the abstract, you make war on language itself; but that is not O'Grady's intention. He wishes to proscribe evasion, pretentiousness, cowardly euphemisms, slack expressions, fuzzy synonyms. The aim is praiseworthy, but the vices levelled at are not found exclusively in abstract words. One may be a bamboozler and a waffler in quite concrete terms. (When a certain Prime Minister assured the British nation that *the pound in your pocket* would not lose its value, he was fooling us all with a homely circumlocution employing good honest concrete nouns. An abstraction – e.g. *your financial resources* – would not have done the job so well.) 'Prefer truth to falsehood' and 'prefer strength to weakness' are moral recommendations of indisputable worth, but they are not conclusively put into force by preferring the concrete to the abstract.

(b) *The passive*

The case against the passive is, first, that its impersonal use is often an evasion of responsibility, and second, that it is apparently less compact, and so less decisive in the impression it leaves, than the active form. Gowers says of the impersonal passive in official letters: 'It gives the reader the impression that he is dealing with robots rather than human beings' (*CPW*,30). H.W. Fowler's dictionary entry on the passive includes the assertion that 'when one person is addressing another it [the passive] *often amounts* to a pusillanimous shrinking from responsibility.' One might add (or, it might be added!) that the passive construction and the abstract noun can be combined in dishonesties of officialspeak: *New proposals for raising revenue are being studied* means 'The Chancellor is thinking up another tax.'

It is also true that passive constructions, in changing the focus of a declarative sentence (see 2.9), may suggest artful contrivance; and that because the passive transformation requires a word or two more than the active form it may seem comparatively slack. Textbook discussions abound in discreetly worded constructions such as *It may be objected that . . ., It will soon be seen that . . ., This has been noted earlier . . ., The subject has been exhaustively treated by Professor X . . .*, etc., where author and reader alike would no doubt prefer the robust directness of *You may object . . ., We shall soon see . . ., I have shown . . ., Professor X has dealt with this.* Here convention gets in the way. Some forms of writing traditionally forbid or inhibit the intrusion of a personality, and thus the impersonal passive is forced upon the writer.

The use of the passive may degenerate into a mere mannerism. The fact remains, however, that the passive is an available construction, one of the resources of English, a potentially useful and at times indispensable option. Without it some awkward technical problems would arise in composition. Here is a sentence from *The King's English*:

> The novice who is told to avoid foreign words, and then observes that these English words are used freely, takes the rule for a counsel of perfection – not accepted by good writers, and certainly not to be accepted by him, who is hard to put to it for the ornament that he feels his matter deserves. (*KE*,36)

In this complex declarative sentence there are no less than five clauses with passive verbs: *(the novice) who is told to avoid; (the English words) are used freely; (counsel) not accepted by good writers; (counsel) certainly not to be accepted by him; (him) who is hard put to it.* As the sentence develops there are shifts of theme and focus necessitating the use of the passive. The Fowlers might of course have redrafted the passage, making all the verbs active:

> Teachers tell the novice to avoid foreign words. He then

observes that people use these English words freely, and takes the rule for a counsel of perfection. Good writers, he thinks, do not accept the counsel, and he will certainly not accept it. He has difficulty enough in finding the ornament that he feels his matter deserves.

Rewriting here reduces the long sentence to somewhat shorter units. This in itself helps to eliminate passives; but if the possibility of such reduction were denied, and the complex dependences of a long sentence were demanded, the passive would certainly make its claim as a convenient option. It is an interesting stylistic problem – and one that has absolutely no moral overtones.

Strunk and White tell their readers to 'use the active voice', but concede that 'this rule does not, of course, mean that the writer should entirely discard the passive voice, which is frequently convenient, and sometimes necessary.' (The rule is thus diluted to 'use the active voice except when you want to use the passive'.) They add: 'the need of making a particular word the subject of the sentence will often . . . determine which voice is to be used.' (In other words, 'change the focus, change the voice'.)

The doctrine of avoiding the passive becomes objectionable when it is presented as a matter of personal integrity. Writings on usage often hint at the 'weakness' of the passive, or give examples of its evasiveness. Quiller-Couch makes avoidance of the passive a touchstone of character. 'By their fruits ye shall know them,' he appears to proclaim in the following passage:

> Generally use transitive verbs, that strike their object; and use them in the active voice, eschewing the stationary passive, with its little auxiliary *is*'s and *was*'s, and its participles getting into the light of your adjectives, which should be few. For, as a rough law, by his use of the straight verb and by his economy of adjectives you can tell a man's style, if it be masculine or neuter, writing or 'composition'. (*AW*,137)

This is meretricious; a showy display of false wisdoms. It begins by recommending yet another preference-avoidance: we are to prefer transitive verbs to intransitive verbs, because transitive verbs in downright fashion 'strike' their object. Some fairly unstriking examples of transitive verbs are *like*, in *I like your ideas*; *expect*, in *I am expecting a message*; *consider*, in *let us consider the problem*; *drop*, in *she dropped a hint*; *find*, in *I couldn't find words*; *develop*, in *the professor developed his argument*; *undergo*, in *Jekyll's appearance undergoes periodic transformations*. There are countless other instances of transitive verbs that 'strike' their objects something less than forcibly. Quiller-Couch appears to have felt, however, that transitivity must be a sinewy, manly process. The one disadvantage of transitive verbs from his point of view is that they can be made passive, and the passive is to be 'eschewed', because it is 'stationary' (so, *two windows were smashed by the builders* comes to a standstill by comparison with *the builders smashed two windows*) because it requires 'little auxiliary' verbs; and because its 'participles get into the light of your adjectives', which, however, 'should be few'.

The statement that participles 'get into the light' of adjectives baffles interpretation. No example is given, and none springs to mind. *Cruel Mr Squeers bullied poor unhappy Smike* can be turned into *Poor unhappy Smike was bullied by cruel Mr Squeers* without the inopportune darkening of a single epithet. *In America, fortunate customers have often been served by smiling, courteous waitresses* makes no more of a participle-dimmed, adjective-cluttered mess than *In America, smiling, courteous waitresses have often served fortunate customers*. There may be times when the passive arguably 'gets into the light' of other constructions, perhaps by complicating the pattern of a complex sentence; equally, there may be times when the passive resolves problems of structure. Quiller-Couch does not look into these possibilities.

His remarks on transitives and passives are so much solemn flapdoodle; or, if that seems too harsh a judgment, let us use one of O'Grady's best-loved strictures, and call them 'muddled thinking'. A verb does not convey a sense of vigour, strength, or manly directness, simply by being transitive; a verb in the passive voice is not 'stationary' (or even *stative* – see 2.4) because it is grammatically passive; 'little auxiliaries' occur not only in the passive, but also in the compound tenses and aspectual forms of verbs in the active voice; turning active into passive can change the focus of a clause or promote the cohesion of a text, but nothing has to 'get into the light' of anything. If these notions from a sixty-year-old text were merely amusing examples of old-fashioned error, there would be little point in attacking them. O'Grady, however, is still saying things like this, and he has disciples who are ready to believe that the passive is an ineffectual bumbler and that transitive verbs demonstrate their virility by striking their objects.

## 8 Into the future, facing hopefully backwards

O'Grady's pronouncements are frequently retrospective; he faces backwards into the future, brooding over the likelihood of things that have already happened. Commenting on words like *asexual* and *amoral* (the progress of which, at the expense of 'the more orthodox non-moral', he regrets), Fowler declares: 'These words should not be treated as precedents for future word-making' (*MEU*,1). 'Should not' is interesting; in sense, it seems to waver between 'must not' and 'ought not'. On the meaning of *cryptic*, Fowler pronounces less emphatically, using 'might' rather than 'should': 'it might be usefully reserved for what is purposely equivocal, like the utterances of the Delphic oracle and not treated as a stylish synonym for *mysterious, obscure, hidden*, and other such words'. On *critique* he is hopeful: 'it is in less common use than it was, and with *review, criticism*, and *notice* ready at need, there is some hope of its dying out, except so far as it may be kept alive by the study of Kant' (*MEU*,114). (Some hope, but not a great deal: in the *Guardian*, 27 July 1984, we read that *One critique . . . has recently come from Lord Kaldor*. More than half a century after Fowler, the word is alive and canting.) On *phenomenal*, however, not used in its strict metaphysical sense, Fowler is mournfully resigned: 'To divert it from its proper use to a job for which it is not needed, by making it do duty for remarkable, extraordinary, or prodigious, was a sin against the English language, but the consequences seem now to be irremediable; this meaning is recognized without comment by most dictionaries' (*MEU*,450)

Wishing that usages had never happened, and would go

away, is an O'Gradyish habit. The triumph of *hopefully* in the sense 'it is to be hoped' (note how the adverb supplants the awkward passive) is a good recent example. In Strunk and White we find:

> HOPEFULLY. This once-useful adverb meaning 'with hope' has been distorted and is now widely used to mean 'I hope', or 'it is to be hoped'. Such use is not merely wrong, it is silly. To say, 'Hopefully I'll leave on the noon plane' is to talk nonsense. Do you mean you'll leave on the noon plane in a hopeful frame of mind? Or do you mean you hope you'll leave on the noon plane? Whichever you mean, you haven't said it clearly. Although the word in its new, free-floating capacity may be pleasurable and even useful to many, it offends the ear of many others, who do not like to see words dulled and eroded, particularly when the erosion leads to ambiguity. (*ES*,48)

The use of *hopefully* to mean 'it is to be hoped' may irritate the conservative, but it is neither 'wrong' nor 'silly'. It is not nonsense, and it does not lead to ambiguity. In writing, a simple act of punctuation distinguishes *hopefully* = 'it is to be hoped' from *hopefully* = 'in a state of hope':

> *To travel hopefully is better than to arrive.*
> (*hopefully* as adverbial adjunct; = 'travelling in hope is better than arriving')

> *To travel, hopefully, is better than to arrive.*
> (*hopefully* as adverbial disjunct, see *Grammar of Contemporary English* 8.50; = 'Let's hope that travelling is better than arriving')

When the disjunct is placed at the beginning of the clause, it is followed by a comma (*Hopefully, to travel is better*, etc.). The adjunct in the initial position takes no comma, but *Hopefully to travel* is the kind of fronting (see 2.5) that is generally restricted to verse or highly rhetorical prose. In speech, intonation and rhythm distinctively 'punctuate' the contrasting forms, and the positioning of the adverb may be critical. *Hopefully I'll leave on the noon plane*, however it may be intoned, virtually dictates the interpretation 'I hope'. The marking of an adverb of manner by giving it first place in the clause (as in *Cheerfully I'll do my duty, Gladly my cross I'd bear*, etc.) is a device of literary or oratorical rhetoric hardly to be expected in conversations about air travel. The recently developed 'capacity' of the disjunct *hopefully* is not 'free-floating'. It is subject to grammatical rule; and though in this sense the word may 'offend the ear' of those 'who do not like to see'(!) the 'erosion' of meaning, it is not in the least 'eroded' or 'dulled'.

Sir Ernest Gowers seems to regret somewhat the spread of *hopefully* as disjunct ('it is of course quite illogical', he says – compelling assent with *of course*). However, his general comments show his usual urbanity and good sense:

> ... it seems to me that the new use of *hopefully* has established itself as a new idiom. The careful writer is now faced with a new duty – to make sure that whenever he uses *hopefully* for either purpose he avoids any ambiguity about which use he intends. (*CPW*,226)

Gowers notes that *thankfully* has 'adopted a similar course', and ventures to predict:

> Other adverbs may follow these examples before long. *Regretfully* is already sometimes used to mean *I regret to say*. But this is rather perverse, because *regrettably* is already available for this meaning. *Hopefully* and *thankfully* can at least claim to be filling a gap left by the absence of *hopeably* and *thankably*. (*CPW*,227)

Here is some attempt, at least, to understand the course of usage, the underlying motives of change, and the possibilities of future development. There is an interesting footnote to this particular case. In 1926, H.W. Fowler, commenting on the verb *hope* (*MEU*, 249–50), drew attention to the meaning 'expect', which is often implicit in that verb. (As in the old story of the felon who said he 'hoped to be hanged'.) Fowler also remarked on the awkwardness of the construction *it is hoped*, and the solecisms resulting from the attempt to use *it is hoped* non-disjunctively. Thus *hope* has the sense 'expect' in *A luncheon at which the King is hoped to be present*, and *it is hoped* is 'falsely' incorporated in *The final arrangements of what is hoped will prove a 'monster demonstration'*. (Read: *The final arrangements of what, it is hoped, will prove a 'monster demonstration'*.) From these two observations – that *hope* often contains the meaning 'expect', and that *it is hoped* is commonly mismanaged – the advent of *hopefully* might almost have been predicted. The need for a clearer construction was already there (*A luncheon at which, hopefully, the King will be present*; *The final arrangements of what, hopefully, will prove a 'monster demonstration'*). But the solution was not available until *hopefully* arrived from German *hoffentlich*, via American English. Then, as Gowers rightly observes, other adverbs began to be comparably treated. Sometimes, if we are alert, we can see how, and understand why, usage changes.

### 9 Under which king?

The question remains – under which king? If we need government at all, what do we look for in the government of usage? There are some who put their faith in particular princes, swearing by Fowler, or Gowers, or Partridge. For others, the king is a phantom ideal, an authority identified less by a real presence than by the inclinations and aspirations of the subject. These inclinations may be characterized:

(a) The need to have clear and exclusive rulings (i.e. of 'right' and 'wrong') on all points of usage.
(b) The impulse to resist any change, but especially change in language.
(c) A dislike of 'exceptions', an aversion to the idea of alternatives being determined by purposes.
(d) The belief that there is a stylistic standard, a convention establishing 'norms' of reference and judgment.

Such are the general feelings of those who like to serve under an absolute rule. On the other hand, some of the governed have more liberal requirements, i.e.:

(a) A need for discussion, explanation, evaluation, of disputed points in usage.
(b) A disposition to accept some changes more readily than others, but not to feel that changes are destroying the language.
(c) A wish to feel that there are alternatives in usage and

style, the choice of which is dictated by context and function.
(d) A tendency to regard the 'standard' style as a convenient fiction or abstraction, and to perceive, in reality, various *styles*.

In this case, the ideal ruler of usage is a relativist and a democrat. Most of us are a little uneasy with either dispensation; with the absolute *must* and *must not*, and with the vague, benevolent relativism of *it all depends what you mean*. Like all O'Gradys, when we set up on our own account we want to have the best of every which way.

In the long run, however, relativism rules. It is not frequently possible, in questions of language, to make confident declarations of 'correctness'. Nor is there much evidence that change in language means corruption, and that things lost through change cannot be replaced. There is always some compensation for whatever passes out of language, or some adjustment of whatever system may be disturbed by its passing. It is many centuries since English had so-called 'dual' personal pronouns, i.e. words signifying 'we two', 'you two'. We may have lost something by their departure, but our pronominal system, and our usage generally, has managed to cover the breach. (In poems and songs, the phrase *you and I* – or *me and you* – or *just the two of us* – is charged with dual intimacy.) That same pronominal system is even now undergoing a new change, with the adjusted use of *their* as a neuter gender-pronoun, obviating the potentially offensive *his* and the clumsy *his or her*. (Compare *Every ratepayer should check his assessment*; *Every ratepayer should check his or her assessment*; *Every ratepayer should check their assessment*.) The same tendency can be observed (it has been apparent for a very long time) in *they*: *When someone has had an operation, they take months to get over it*. Because the use of *they* and *their* sometimes forces on the user a sense of false agreement, there is a current tendency to put nouns denoting occupation, function, etc., into the plural: *Authors should check their proofs carefully*, *Applicants are to be informed of their rights*. These tendencies do not yet amount to a change, in the sense of a newly standardized usage; they exist, for the time being, as definable symptoms of a social feeling When this usage is finally tidied into the manuals of grammar, it may be that we shall mourn some loss of precision, some blurring of reference; but we shall have gained something in return, something required by the public will. In one small respect our language will be more fairly representative of the society it is intended to serve.

As to style, the notion of a standard, or 'middle', is one that rhetoricians have been propounding since classical times. In its English form, the doctrine of the middle style is a precept of gentlemanly accomplishment – affable, well-bred, artlessly artful, unpedantically correct. The ideal of a 'normal texture of English prose' is expounded by G. H. Vallins, commenting on Hazlitt's term, 'familiar style':

> It is a formal artistic counterpart, and indeed development, of the personal artless style. The writer trims his sentence to an accepted syntactical pattern, subject and predicate with the modification of clause and phrase, filling up the common ellipses of the spoken word; suggests by turns of expression the emphases and gestures of ordinary talk; uses a vocabulary that is at once intelligible, interesting, and evocative; and so varies his constructions that he avoids the effect of monotony. He gives coherence to speech, at the same time retaining certain of its characteristics. His immediate appeal is through the eye of the reader; but he does not forget the reader's ear. (*BE*, 166–7)

This really tells us very little about the 'normal texture of English prose', apart from suggesting that sentences should have subjects and verbs, that the vocabulary should be interesting, and that rhythm is important. What it affirms is the traditional view of a relationship between writing (superior) and speaking (subordinate). Style, it suggests, is in effect groomed conversation. 'An accepted syntactical pattern' does not imply the menace of the asyntactic (e.g. *On sat cat the mat the*), but simply that in writing one ought not to skip subjects, drop verbs, forget antecedents, or slide out of one construction into another. Writers (Vallins would argue) like to have the sense of talking to someone, and because 'someone' is a stranger, they ought to mind their verbal manners. Indeed they ought; but that is not the whole story of style, and certainly not of *styles*. There are writings that bear little resemblance to polite and private interactions – writings that address a public, that express the functions of social and political institutions, that expound and criticize the roles we play in life. Writing has social contexts from which it can hardly be dissociated, and every context has requirements of style.

To be convinced of a right answer, a single way, a universal principle, may be very comforting, but the demand for these things ignores the complexities of usage and amounts to a rejection of a style – for if the rules of writing were as certain and immutable as the patterns of Ciceronian prose, we might all rest easy in our well-trimmed plots in the dead middle-ground of expression. The hidden principles are more exacting than that. They ascribe to the user the capacity to judge and decide, the responsibility for ascertaining facts, perceiving alternatives, making choices, learning from mistakes. It is not easy; but if we serve under this king there can be no affront to our humanity, no sense of being tried and rejected, only the fascinating variety of speech, and the endlessly gratifying difficulty of writing. And that, for the time being, is all that we can ask.

# Bibliography

The writings on English usage are numerous. This is a short list, for reference or further reading. Some of these works have been recurrently cited, notably in Chapter 6, where the following abbreviations have been used:

KE    Fowler, H.W. and Fowler, F.G., *The King's English*.
MEU    Fowler, H.W., *A Dictionary of Modern English Usage*.
CPW    Gowers, Sir Ernest, *The Complete Plain Words*.
CE    Orwell, George, *Collected Essays*, vol. IV.
UA    Partridge, Eric, *Usage and Abusage*.
AW    Quiller-Couch, Sir Arthur, *The Art of Writing*.
ES    Strunk, W. and White, E.B., *The Elements of Style*.
BE    Vallins, G.H., *Better English*.

*On grammar*

Close, R.A, *A Reference Grammar for Students of English* London, Longman, 1975.

Quirk, Randolph, Greenbaum, Sidney, Leech, Geoffrey, and Svartrik, Jan, *A Grammar of Contemporary English*, London, Longman, 1972.

Quirk, Randolph, and Greenbaum, Sidney, *A University Grammar of English*, London, Longman, 1973.

Quirk, Randolph, Greenbaum, Sidney, Leech, Geoffrey, and Svartvik, Jan, *A Comprehensive Grammar of English*, London, Longman, 1985.

*On language and society*

Milroy, J., and Milroy, L., *Authority in Language: Approaches to Language Standardisation and Prescription*, London, Routledge & Kegan Paul, 1985.

Stubbs, M., *Language and Literacy*, London, Routledge & Kegan Paul, 1980.

*On usage*
Cottle, Basil, *The Plight of English: Ambiguities, Cacophonies, and other Violations of Our Language*, Newton Abbot, David & Charles, 1975. (This authoritarian text is well written, sometimes with provocative wit, and raises some interesting issues.)
Crystal, David, *Who Cares about English Usage?*, London, Penguin Books, 1984. (Based on Professor Crystal's radio broadcasts, and on correspondence from listeners.)
Evans, Sir Ifor, 'The Nature and Use of Direct English', in *The Use of English*, London, McGibbon & Kee, 2nd edn, 1966. (Proposes a reform of the language of government and administration, through the introduction of Direct English. 'Direct English' is defined as 'the use of English, preserving the natural idiom of the language with a close regard to lucidity and brevity.' No technical criteria are stated; the author makes frequent appeal to 'clarity', 'logic', and 'the arrangement of thought'. Direct English, he says, 'should be applied on all occasions when a cost factor and a time factor make brevity desirable.' (Use it when you want to save time and money). The benefits of Direct English are illustrated by the adroit rewriting of several passages of officialese.)
Fowler, H.W. and Fowler, F.G., *The King's English*, London, Oxford University Press, 3rd edn, paperback reprint, 1979. (First published 1906.)
Fowler, H.W. *A Dictionary of Modern English Usage*, Oxford, Clarendon Press, 2nd edn, revised by Sir Ernest Gowers, 1965. (First published 1926.)
Gowers, Sir Ernest, *The Complete Plain Words*, London, Penguin Books, 2nd edn revised by Sir Bruce Fraser, repr. 1979. (First published in 1948. This is a compendium of two earlier books, *Plain Words* and *The ABC of Plain Words*, written with the aim of improving official English.)
Orwell, George, 'Politics and the English Language', in *The Collected Essays, Journalism and Letters of George Orwell*, vol. IV, ed: S. Orwell and I. Angus, London, Secker &

Warburg, 1968. (This essay, more than anything else written in this century, has established the respectable and sometimes inflexible conviction that plain English is good English and good English is plain English. Two syllables good, four syllables bad.)

Partridge, Eric, *Usage and Abusage*, London, Hamish Hamilton, 1947. (Reprinted Penguin Books, 1963. Citations in the present text are from the 1947 edition.)

Quirk, Randolph, *The Use of English*, London, Longman, 2nd edn, 1968.

Strunk, W. and White, E.B., *The Elements of Style*, 3rd edn, New York, Macmillan Publishing Co., 1979. (A prescriptive best-seller. The most useful part of the work is the final chapter, by White, entitled 'An Approach to Style'.)

Vallins, G.H. *Good English: How to Write It*, London, Pan Books, 1951.

Vallins, G.H., *Better English*, London, Andre Deutsch, 1955. (first published Pan Books, 1953.)

Warburg, Jeremy, *Verbal Values*, London, Edward Arnold, 1966. (This little book deserves to be better known. It consists of three dialogues, in the form of tutorial discussions between teacher and pupil. These conversations on English usage are entitled 'Good and Bad', 'Plain and Unplain', and 'Correct and Incorrect'. The dialogue on 'Plain and Unplain' usefully criticizes 'the tendency to equate good English with terms such as *plain* or *clear*, and bad English with terms such as *unplain* or *obscure*. Partly because the senses of the terms are uncertain. But quite apart from this, just because they're 'false equations'.)

Weiner, E.S.C., *The Oxford Guide to English Usage*, London, Oxford University Press, 1983. (Also issued, 1984, as *The Oxford Guide to the English Language*, in this format including a dictionary compiled by Joyce M. Hawkins. The guide to usage contains sections on word formation, the pronunciation of words, words habitually misused, and the elements of grammar.)

*On rhetoric and composition*

Brooks, Cleanth, and Warren, Robert Penn, *Modern Rhetoric*, New York, Harcourt Brace Jovanovich, shorter 3rd edn, 1972.

Dillon, George L., *Constructing Texts: Elements of a Theory of Composition and Style*, Bloomington, Indiana University Press, 1981.

Graves, Robert, and Hodge, Alan, *The Reader over Your Shoulder*, Jonathan Cape, 1943. (Sub-titled *A Handbook for Writers of English Prose*, this is remarkable for the detail of its critical prescriptiveness. It minutely analyses the faults of selected passages by famous contemporaries (e.g. T.S. Eliot, J.M. Keynes, J.B. Priestley, I.A. Richards, Bertrand Russell, G.B. Shaw, H.G. Wells) and presents so-called 'fair copies', i.e. corrected versions. To read it is a chastening and perhaps somewhat discouraging experience.)

Nash, Walter, *Designs in Prose: A Study of Compositional Problems and Methods*, London, Longman, 1980.

Tufte, V., *Grammar as Style*, New York, Holt, Rinehart & Winston, 1971. (Excellent for its close study of grammatical resources and their use by modern writers, American and British.)

*On punctuation and presentation*

Carey, G.V., *Mind the Stop: A Brief Guide to Punctuation with a Note on Proof-Correction*, London, Penguin Books, 1980. (First published Cambridge University Press, 1939.)

Maney, A.S., and Smallwood, R.L. (eds), *MHRA Style Book: Notes for Authors, Editors and Writers of Dissertations*, London, for the Modern Humanities Research Association, 2nd edn, 1978.

Partridge, Eric, *You Have a Point There: A Guide to Punctuation and its Allies*, London, Hamish Hamilton, 1953.

Perrin, Porter, G., and Smith, George H., *Handbook of Current English*, Glenview, Illinois, Scott Foresman and Company, 3rd edn revised by Jim W. Corder, 1968. (This excellent work is a comprehensive handbook, with a detailed treatment of grammar, usage, punctuation and other conventions in writing, and many aspects of composition. It stresses the principle of *appropriateness* in usage and style. Written for American college students, it is unfortunately not easily available to British readers.)

van Leunen, Mary-Claire, *A Handbook for Scholars*, New York, Alfred A. Knopf, 1979.

# Index

'abstractitis', 144
abstract words, 143–7
active voice, as stylistic option, 43, 50, 86, 140, 141, 148, 150
address, stylistic options of, *see* options
adverb, 21, 37, 74
adverbial [*A*], sentence element, 17, 21, 39
   location of, 25–6
   manner, 36
   place, 26
   time, 26
adverbial clause, *see* clause
*advertisement* (accentuation of), 7, 8
agent, 28, 87
agreement (concord), 55–6
à Kempis, Thomas, 96
ambiguity, 12–13, 59–60, 126
Amis, Kingsley, 129
*amoral*, 151
antecedent, antecedence, 52, 59, 60, 85, 107–8, 119, 124
antimetabole (chiasmus), 96
apposition, 118
appropriateness, as style criterion, 10
*asexual*, 151
aspect (in grammar), 20
Athill, Diana, 1
attitude, 'scored' by punctuation, 107–9
auxiliary verb, 20

Bacon, Francis, 73

'Of Studies', 97–9
'book-style', 90–2
Brain, Sir Russell:
   *The Nature of Experience*, 49
brackets, *see* punctuation
branching, 38, 50
   as stylistic option, 78, 81–3, 93–4, 104
Burns, Robert, 15
'by-phrase' (in the passive, *q.v.*), 28–9, 87

change in language, 5–9
   diversity of change, 9
   the 'gossip' of change, 7–9
chiasmus (antimetabole), 96
Churchill, Sir Winston, 63
*cigarette* (accentuation of), 8
clarity, as style criterion, 10
clause, 29–44:
   adverbial, 39, 44, 61, 62–3, 119, 124
   dependent (subordinate), 35, 60, 112
   embedded, 32
   independent, 35
   infinitive, 36, 44, 57, 94, 121
   non-finite, 36, 57
   noun clause, 122
   participle, 36, 44, 60, 115, 120
   principal (main), 36, 60, 62
   relative, 'non-restrictive', 108–119
   relative, 'restrictive', 108, 119
   verbless, 36–7, 60, 115, 119
   wh-clause, in the pseudo-cleft

# Index

sentence, *q.v.*, 31; as sentence subject, or object, 32, 39; and punctuation, 122–3
  *see also* sentence patterns
cleft sentence, 30, 43
  *see also* focus, postpositioning
coherence, as style criterion, 46–9
cohesion, textual, 40–2
*cohort*, 8
colon, *see* punctuation
comma, *see* punctuation
comment (grammatical/semantic term), 13, 27, 31
  *see also* focus, order of clauses, postpositioning
compactness, as style criterion, 52–3
complement [$C$], sentence element:
  subject complement [$C_s$], 17, 21, 22, 23, 39, 58, 79
  object complement [$C_o$], 17, 22, 39
  *see also* focus; fronting; marked construction; theme
complementation, 20–2
  intensive, 21, 23
  extensive, 21
'completive' pattern (stylistic option), 81
complex sentence, *see* sentence patterns
concord (agreement), 55–6, 58
concrete words, 140, 144–7
conjunct, 82, 118, 134
conjunction, 33, 34, 36, 64, 74, 104, 117, 135
'constrictive' and 'constructive' responses to usage, 10–11
*controversy* (accentuation of), 7, 8
coordination, 33, 117–18
coordinator, 34
*court card*, 7
Cowper, William, 72
*critique*, 151

*Daily Telegraph*, 46, 56, 58, 66
'dangling participle', 60
dash, *see* punctuation
declarative sentence form, 18
  as stylistic option, 43, 88
dependent (subordinate) clause, *see* clause
Dickens, Charles, 7
direct object [$O_d$], sentence element, *see* object
discretion, as style criterion, 53–5
disjunct, 37, 60, 62, 82, 118
distributive options, in style, *see* options
ditransitive, 22
dynamic (semantic property of verb), 24, 58

elements of simple sentence, 17
  order of elements, 24–5
  *see also* adverbial; complement; object; subject; verb
embedding, 32, 38–40, 44, 57, 94
  as stylistic option, 76–7
embedded clause, *see* clause
enumeratives, 118
exclamation point, *see* punctuation
exclamations, in 'speech-style', *q.v.*, 91
existential sentence, 29, 43
  *see also* focus, postpositioning
'expansion' (stylistic option), 76–8
extensive complementation, *see* complementation
extraposition, 30, 31, 43
  *see also* focus, postpositioning

*face card*, 7
fashions, repudiation of (as style criterion), 10
felicity (as style criterion), 10
focus, 13, 27–8
  end-focus, 27, 28, 29–30, 84–5, 88
  mid-branching and focus, 38
  shifts of focus, 31–2
  *see also* comment; fronting; postpositioning; theme; topic
formal/conventional (denoting stylistic option), 92
Fowler, F.G. and Fowler, H.W.: *The King's English* (Fowler F.G. and H.W.), 54, 129, 131, 132–3, 137, 139, 140, 142

# Index

*A Dictionary of Modern English Usage* (Fowler H.W.), 137, 144, 147, 151, 153–4
fronting, 25
  see also focus, theme, topic
front-heaviness (front-weighting), 57, 77, 87
  see also order of clauses
full stop, see punctuation

*garage* (pronunciation of), 8
gender pronoun, 8
gender suffix, 8
Gowers, Sir Ernest:
  *Plain Words*, 129
  *The Complete Plain Words*, 130, 141, 142, 145, 147, 153–4
grammar, of sentences, 15–44
  constructive value of grammar, 14
Graves, Robert, 100
*Guardian*, 53, 54, 60, 80, 151

*harass* (accentuation of), 8
Hazlitt, William, 45
head (of noun phrase, *q.v.*), 18
Hemingway, Ernest:
  *Death in the Afternoon*, 115
  *The Old Man and the Sea*, 62, 123
*hopefully*, 37, 152–4
*however* (position as conjunct), 133–4

idiom, 14, 65
idiomatic logic, 65
independent clause, see clause
indirect object [$O_i$], see object
infinitive clause, see clause
informal/familiar (denoting stylistic option), 92
'insiders' and 'outsiders' (defined by usage), 137–40
intensifier, 91, 94, 134
intensive complementation, see complementation
'interruptive' pattern (stylistic option), 81
intransitive, 23, 149–51

*jack* (playing card), 1, 7, 8, 14
jargon, 68, 144
Jerome, Jerome K:
  *Three Men in a Boat*, 111
Johnson, Dr Samuel, 2, 5, 6, 97–9
  *The Rambler*, 2, 99

*kilometre* (accentuation of), 8
*King Henry IV, Part II*, 129
*knave* (playing card), 7

Langland, William, 15
*launch* (pronunciation of), 7
*lay* (collocating with *table*), 7
left-branching, see branching
'level of address' (stylistic), 92
  see also options of address; usage and style
lexical verb, see verb
Lincoln, Abraham:
  *The Gettysburg Address*, 96, 116

main (principal) clause, see clause
'malaprops' (Fowlerian term), 132
marked construction, 25, 28, 43, 84, 87
  see also comment; focus; fronting; theme; topic
*marriage* (pronunciation of), 8
metaphor, mixed, 66
modal auxiliary, 20
  see also verb
moral constructions, in 'book-style', *q.v.*, 91–5
*modern-day*, 6
modifier, 18
Moliere, Jean Baptiste, 96
mood (in grammar), 19
  see also modal constructions
mid-branching, see branching
*Midsummer Night's Dream, A*, 100
myths, prescriptive, 133–7

na Gopaleen, Myles (Flann O'Brien, Brian O'Nolan):
  *Catechism of Cliché*, 69
negation, use of, in 'book-style', *q.v.*, 91, 94–5
*New Statesman*, 65

*New Yorker*, 115, 130
nominal item, 18
non-finite clause, *see* clause
noun, 18, 54
noun phrase, 18–19, 21, 57, 83, 88, 89, 96, 99, 115
*nowadays*, 5
number (in the verb), 55

object, sentence element:
   direct object [$O_d$], 17, 21, 22, 24, 25, 39
   indirect object [$O_i$], 17, 22, 25, 39
   *see also* focus, fronting, marked construction, theme
object complement [$C_o$], *see* complement
O'Grady, (authority symbol), 129–57 *passim*
options (in style):
   distributive options, 74–83
   presentative options, 84–90
   options of address, 90–9
   *see also* active voice; 'book-style'; branching; 'completive' pattern; declarative sentence form; embedding; expansion; familiar/conventional; fronting; informal/familiar; passive voice; paraphrase; postpositive sentence form; punctuation; rhetorical patterning; sentence length; 'speech-style'
order of clauses, 34–6, 38, 78–88
   *see also* branching; 'completive' pattern; 'interruptive' pattern; postpositioning
Orwell, George:
   'Politics and the English Language', 140–1, 143

paraphrase, as stylistic option, 95–9
parenthesis:
   example of confusing parenthesis, 62–3
   punctuation of parenthetical clauses, 119, 125

stylistic value of parenthesis, 83, 127–8
Partridge, Eric:
   *Usage and Abusage*, 1, 6, 11, 130, 134, 135, 138, 139, 154
passive voice:
   in 'book-style' (*q.v.*), 90
   as focusing device, 28–9, 31
   as stylistic option, 43, 50, 86–7, 89, 112, 140, 141, 147–51
perfective, *see* aspect
postmodification, 18–19
postpositioning, 29–31
   *see also* comment; focus; topic
'postpositive' sentence form, as stylistic option, 88
   use in 'book-style', 90
precepts, Polonian, 140–2
premodification, 18–19
prescription(s), 3–4, 5, 6, 55–72, 130–3
   *see also* myths, prescriptivism, received myths, retrospective prescriptions
'prescriptivism', principles summarized, 154
presentative options, in style, *see* options
*present-day*, 6
preposition, 59
principal (main) clause, *see* clause
progressive, *see* aspect
pronominal system, tendencies to change in, 155
pronoun, personal, 18, 59
   'dual' (historical) forms, 155
   use in 'speech-style' (*q.v.*), 90
   *see also* agreement, antecedents
pseudo-cleft sentence, 31
   *see also* comment, focus, postpositioning, topic
punctuation:
   *marks of:*
   bracket, 125–6
   colon, 112–13
   comma, 115–23, 125–6
   dash, 108, 125
   dot, triple, 60, 125
   exclamation point, 108

full stop, 110–12
quotation marks, 126–7
semi-colon, 113–15
*categories of:*
'scorings', 126–8
stops, 109–26
'suspensions', 134–6
'zero' punctuation, 104, 105, 121, 123–4
*stylistics of:*
as a creative principle, 100–7, 114–15
'comma style', 101
expressing attitudes, 108–9
implications of tone, tempo, &c., 101–3, 108–9, 125
making sense, 107–8
options in punctuation, 104–6, 117
'semi-colon style', 101

questions, direct, in 'speech-style', *q.v.*, 91
Quiller-Couch, Sir Arthur:
*On the Art of Writing*, 140, 144, 146, 149–50

realization (of sentence elements), 16–20, 57–8
received wisdoms, 142–3
relative clause, *see* clause
'relativism', principles summarized, 154–5
repertoire, grammatical, 42–4
retrospective prescription, 151–3
rhetorical patterning, as stylistic option, 95–9
rhythm, 76
right-branching, *see* branching
Ross, Harold, 115

semi-colon, *see* punctuation
sentence length, 74–6
sentence patterns, 15–44
simple sentence, 16–31, 43, 74–6, 84
complex sentence, 15–16, 32–40, 46, 74–6

*see also* distributive options; paraphrase; presentative options; punctuation as creative principle; rhetorical patterning
*serviette*, 7, 8
*set* (in collocation with *table*), 7
scorings, *see* punctuation
Sheridan, R.B., 45
simplicity, as style criterion, 49–51
slang, 68
'sociologese', 144
speaking and writing, 2–5, 156–7
*Spectator*, 62, 68
'speech-style', 90–2
standard, in literary style, 130, 156–7
*see also* usage and style
slative (semantic property of verb), 24, 58
*staunch* (pronunciation of), 7
stops, *see* punctuation
Strunk, W, and White, E.B.:
*The Elements of Style*, 130, 133, 134, 135, 136, 137, 141, 142, 149, 152
'stumpwords', 68
style, *see* usage and style
subject [S], sentence element, *see* complement
subordinate (dependent) clause, *see* clause
subordination, 35–8
subordinator, 35
suspensions, *see* punctuation
Swift, Jonathan, 5

*table napkin*, 8
tag-phrases, 118
*Teaching at a Distance* (Open University publication), 52
*telecaster*, 6
tense, 19
Tennyson, Alfred Lord, 109
text, structure of, 40–2, 48, 49
theme (grammatical/semantic term), 13, 27–8
*see also* comment; focus; order of elements; topic

## Index

Thurber, James:
   *The Years with Ross*, 115–16
*Times, The*, 51, 61, 77, 95
topic (in grammar), 13, 27, 31, 84
transitive, 22
transitivity, 22–3, 149–51
   *see also* complementation
TV news transmissions, cited, 60–1

understatement, 91, 95
unmarked construction, 25, 43
usage and style, 4–5
   criteria of, 10–11
   determinants of style, 45
   elusiveness of criteria, 11–14
   'first level' and 'second level'
     problems, 45–6, 71–2, 73
   literary standard, 156–7
   style as interaction, 5, 71, 90
   usage and social class, 131
usage trap, 1–14

Vallins, G.H.:
   *Better English*, 156
verb [*V*], sentence element, 16, 19, 20, 21, 22, 23–4

agreement (concord), 55–6
auxiliary verb, 20
dynamic verb, 24
infinitive, 36, 122
lexical verb, 20
modal auxiliary, 20, 49
stative verb, 24
*see also* active voice; aspect;
   mood; number; passive voice;
   tense; transitivity; verb phrase
verbless clause, *see* clause
verb phrase, 20
vocabulary, 65–71
   in 'book-style' and 'speech-style'
     (*q.v.*), 92

Waugh, Evelyn:
   *Edmund Campion*, 100–7
wh-clause, *see* clause
*while*, 135–7
Woolf, Virginia:
   *Mrs Dalloway*, 127–8

Young, G.M., 144

zero punctuation, *see* punctuation

For Product Safety Concerns and Information please contact our EU representative GPSR@taylorandfrancis.com
Taylor & Francis Verlag GmbH, Kaufingerstraße 24, 80331 München, Germany